Trees

Trees

Essential know-how and expert advice for gardening success

CONTENTS

A bright red-leaved Japanese maple (*Acer palmatum*) creates a focal point all year round in this small garden.

WHY PLANT A TREE?

Trees are the linchpins of any garden design, their elegant network of stems and leafy canopies providing structure, color, and texture all year round. There's a tree for every garden size and style, too, ranging from towering woodland species suitable for large plots to tiny fruit trees that can be housed in a patio pot. Trees also play an essential role in maintaining healthy ecosystems by supporting a wide range of insects, birds, and mammals, while their ability to store carbon helps mitigate the effects of climate change.

TREES FOR ALL

Trees bring a multitude of benefits to gardens of all sizes, providing height, structure, color, and texture, along with cool shade on hot summer days. Flowers, leaves, and fall berries add to their aesthetic value. It is perhaps because of their visual allure that trees have also been shown to raise our spirits and improve our mental health. Aside from their ornamental value, trees are invaluable to wildlife, too, providing food and homes for insects, birds, and small garden animals. They also absorb carbon and help counter the effects of global warming.

SIZING UP THE BENEFITS

Whatever your garden's size or shape, there is a choice of trees to suit it. You can even grow one in a large pot on a balcony or roof terrace if you're prepared to water it regularly.

Some trees, such as the Juneberry (*Amelanchier laevis*) and cornelian cherry (*Cornus mas*), are naturally compact and ideal for small gardens, while others, including apple and pear trees, are available grafted on to dwarfing rootstocks to restrict their size.

At the other end of the scale, if you have more space, you may want a larger, stately specimen tree that will give height and structure, such as the tulip tree (*Liriodendron tulipifera*), with its handsome lobed foliage and cup-shaped summer flowers, or the elegant, spreading saucer magnolia (*Magnolia* × *soulangeana*).

In between these two extremes there lies a wealth of beautiful garden trees that will grace your space with their foliage, flowers, and fruits. This book offers a carefully curated selection of ornamental and productive trees for a wide range of garden sizes and styles to help you to select the right one for your plot.

The Juneberry tree is naturally compact and produces white spring blossoms and fiery autumn leaves.

DECIDUOUS VS. EVERGREEN

Trees light up the garden throughout the year with their evolving array of colorful flowers, leaves, and stems. Choose a deciduous tree if you want to celebrate the glory of the changing seasons, from spring blossoms to fall colors, and bare winter stems that form a network of filigree patterns to enliven the cold, dark months. Evergreens have their place, too, offering a permanent backdrop of leaf color all year round, and some, such as holly (*Ilex*), also produce seasonal berries and flowers.

Choose a deciduous tree such as a magnolia to fill your garden with pollen-rich flowers each spring.

Apple blossoms provide a source of nectar for bees and other pollinators in a wildlife garden in the spring.

MOOD-ENHANCERS

Trees are beautiful garden plants, but enjoyment of their appearance is not the only benefit they offer us. Recent research has concluded that walking among trees, or simply looking at them, can improve our mental health, too. An Australian study showed that people living in urban areas have a lower risk of developing psychological distress and enjoy better overall health if they have more trees within a walkable distance from their homes. The researchers say that the colors, natural shapes, and textures, as well as the scents and rustling of leaves in the breeze, distract us from our daily stresses, keeping us calm and improving our mental well-being. Other research has shown that trees and green spaces help improve memory and concentration levels. This stack of research provides another good reason to include a tree or two in your yard.

The colors, textures, and details of a tree distract us from our worries and help lower stress levels.

DEFINING A STYLE

Trees can be used to help augment a design theme, such as a Japanese-style garden, where a graceful maple (*Acer palmatum*) will provide a colorful focal point. If you are creating a wildlife garden, you could try a heritage apple or a hedgerow tree, such as *Acer campestre*, or in an herb garden, consider clipped bay to add height and structure. A yard used by a young family may simply need a pretty tree that offers shade over a seating or play area to keep the children cool and prevent sunburn. In a front yard, a compact species that can tolerate pollution and won't cast too much shade over the house would be a good choice—a small hawthorn such as *Crataegus persimilis* 'Prunifolia Splendens' fits the bill, and studies show it can also trap tiny airborne pollution particles.

WHAT IS A TREE?

Knowing the functions of different parts of a tree and how it feeds and grows will help you understand how to keep it healthy. A common misconception is that the roots grow as a mirror image of the tree above the ground, when, in fact, most roots are in the top 3¼–6ft (1–2m) of soil, where there are plenty of nutrients and moisture. If you are planting close to buildings, ask your nursery how far the root system of your tree is likely to develop, so that you can decide where best to plant it. When planting, take care not to damage the trunk, which is the pipeline for the tree's water and food supplies.

Hazel (*Corylus avellana*) is an example of a shrublike tree with multiple trunks.

THE DEFINITION OF A TREE

Trees are tall plants with woody trunks and stems, but shrubs can also fit this description, and the definition of each is not always clear, with treelike shrubs and shrublike trees blurring the distinction between the two. However, trees are generally categorized as having a single trunk (although some do have more than one) and a crown of leaves above that, while shrubs tend to be multi-stemmed and do not grow as large as most trees.

A tree usually has a single trunk and a crown or canopy of leaves above it, as illustrated by this *Stewartia*.

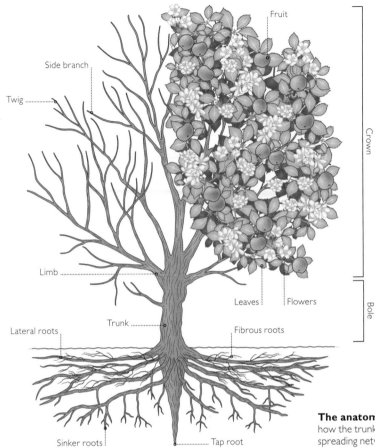

Fruit

Side branch

Twig

Crown

Limb

Leaves Flowers

Bole

Trunk

Lateral roots

Fibrous roots

Sinker roots Tap root

DOWN TO THE ROOTS

Above the ground, a tree comprises a trunk, or bole, which supports side branches, also known as limbs, and a network of smaller branches that grow from them. Smaller still are the twigs, the most recent year's stems, which hold the leaves, flowers, and fruits. If you look up into a tree canopy in summer, you will see how the growth of the twigs is such that all the leaves are held up to the sun.

The roots of a tree absorb water and nutrients from the soil to sustain growth and act as anchors to secure it in the ground. Most trees with a healthy root system will look somewhat like a wine glass, with a broad spread of roots supporting the trunk and crown. Fibrous roots reach into the top layers of soil to take up water and dissolved nutrients, while lateral, sinker, and tap roots stabilize the tree. Take care not to damage the fibrous roots near the surface or to cut through the larger, stabilizing roots.

The anatomy of a typical tree shows how the trunk and canopy relate to the spreading network of roots.

HOW TREES FEED AND GROW

Trees need water and nutrients to stay healthy, but they also require energy, which is provided by sugar produced in the leaves during photosynthesis. This is the process by which trees and other plants use the energy from the sun to convert carbon dioxide (CO_2) absorbed from the air through their leaves and water taken up by the roots into a form of sugar called glucose. The by-product of photosynthesis is oxygen, which is released back into the air. This ability to draw in large volumes of CO_2 and exhale oxygen explains why trees are often described as the "lungs" of the planet. The glucose produced during photosynthesis moves through the tree down the phloem, or live bark, in the stems and trunk. Meanwhile, water and nutrients are transported from the roots to the leaves, flowers, and fruits through the sapwood, which is made up of tubelike tissue called xylem. The phloem is constantly being replenished, and the old cells die off to form the tree's dead bark, which creates a protective sheath around the trunk and stems. The cambium layer (a ring of cells between the phloem and sapwood) is where the lateral growth of a tree takes place, while the area in the center of the trunk, known as the heartwood, is dead wood that stores sugar and keeps the trunk stable and upright.

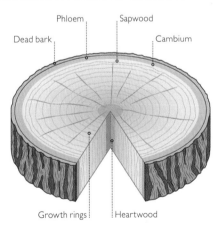

Phloem Sapwood

Dead bark

Cambium

Growth rings Heartwood

A tree's rings indicate its annual growth; the width of the spaces between them shows when conditions were good or bad.

SHAPING UP

Trees come in all shapes and sizes, offering plenty of choices for all yards, large and small. When making your selection, it is a good idea to check what shape a tree will form when mature as well as how tall it will grow to ensure that it will fit your space comfortably. Tall, slim trees are sometimes better suited to small yards than short, wide specimens that may shade more area or grow over the boundary into a neighboring property. The symbols shown opposite and in the tree directories in the book give an indication of the shape a tree will develop.

The crab apple *Malus* 'Evereste' forms a beautiful spreading tree that isn't very tall, but its broad shape takes up quite a lot of space.

SPACE TO GROW

The details about each tree in the directories in this book include one or two of the icons opposite, which refer to its shape. When considered together with the height and spread, they will help you gauge the space a tree requires and the best place to plant it. It is also worth noting that not all trees from one genus, such as a *Malus* or *Prunus*, will develop identical shapes, so read nursery websites carefully for information on the species or cultivar you have chosen. Differences occur because a species may have evolved to suit a particular set of growing conditions, which has affected its habit.

Plant breeders play a role, too, and have developed cultivars that are suited to a range of outdoor situations and design styles. For example, *Prunus sargentii* is a relatively large, rounded tree, while *P. pendula* is a small species with a graceful weeping habit, and *P.* 'Spire', as the name suggests, has an upright, columnar shape, which would provide privacy in a small yard without occupying too much space.

The golden yew (*Taxus baccata* 'Standishii') is a compact form with a distinctive columnar shape.

ALTERED STATES

Trees grown in plenty of light and with space to stretch out their limbs will generally form their predicted shape, but other factors can alter their course. Planting close to an obstruction, such as a tall wall or fence that casts shade on the tree, can result in lopsided growth as the limbs stretch toward the light.

Pruning may also alter the shape of a tree, and those that lend themselves to clipping, such as bay trees (*Laurus nobilis*), can be sculpted into a variety of forms. Trees can also change shape as they grow; they may be rounded when young, then more conical as they age.

A bay tree can be clipped to create a neat lollipop, which is very different from the shape it would naturally make.

CLASSIFYING TREES BY THEIR SHAPE

The descriptions and symbols here denote the main tree shapes and offer an indication of how a species will look when mature. You may find that when your young tree is delivered, it bears little resemblance to the shape on the label or description, but do take note of this because it will soon start to reach up and out to create its natural form, and you will need to provide sufficient space to accommodate it.

ROUNDED TO BROADLY SPREADING This is one of the most common tree shapes and includes *Amelanchier lamarckii* and many popular *Magnolia*, *Malus*, and *Prunus* species.

ROUNDED TO BROADLY COLUMNAR The tulip tree *Liriodendron tulipifera* (pictured below) is one of the best examples of this shape, although there is often little distinction between this and rounded or columnar trees.

BROADLY COLUMNAR Trees with this upright shape include the small-leaved lime (*Tilia cordata*), and some species and cultivars of beech (*Fagus*), maple (*Acer*), and yew (*Taxus*).

NARROWLY COLUMNAR A popular shape for a small space, narrowly columnar trees include cultivars of the conifer *Juniperus scopulorum* and *Liquidambar styraciflua* 'Slender Silhouette', among others.

BROADLY CONICAL *Ginkgo biloba*, hollies (*Ilex*), and many conifers develop a broadly conical shape, and the shorter species and cultivars can make good specimens for small spaces.

FLAME-SHAPED Slim but slightly broader in the center, *Carpinus betulus* 'Fastigiata' (*pictured below*) and the mountain ash *Sorbus* 'Autumn Spire' are good examples of flame-shaped trees.

NARROWLY CONICAL Slim, conical trees, such as the Italian cypress *Cupressus sempervirens*, are ideal for small spaces. Also look out for cultivars of other conifers that create this distinctive shape.

LARGE WEEPING The most famous examples of this tree shape are the weeping willows (*Salix*, pictured below), while the weeping birch (*Betula pendula*) also has pendulous stems.

SMALL WEEPING A few cultivars of larger trees have been bred to form this graceful shape, including the goat willow *Salix caprea* 'Kilmarnock' and *Robinia pseudoacacia* 'Lace Lady'.

MULTI-STEMMED TREE Some shrublike trees, such as hazels, can naturally form this vaselike shape, while others can be pruned when young to create this form.

SINGLE-STEMMED PALM, CYCAD, OR SIMILAR TREE Many palm trees produce a single stem, with elegant fronds fanning out from the top of it. *Trachycarpus fortunei* is one of the best hardy palms with this shape.

The tulip tree *Liriodendron tulipifera*

Carpinus betulus 'Fastigiata'

Weeping willow *Salix babylonica*

CELEBRATE THE SEASONS

Year-round color is a top priority for those with small- to medium-sized gardens, and there is a wide range of trees available that provide leaf color, blossom, fruit, or ornamental bark that will light up each season. If you have space for just one tree, choose a specimen that offers multiple seasons of interest, such as spring blossoms and fall berries, as well as a network of beautiful bare branches in winter. See pp.86–107 for trees that are at their best at a particular time of year and, if you have room for more than one, select a couple that will provide a succession of color and interest.

Pink buds open to reveal white blossoms on an apple tree in spring.

EVOLVING PERFORMANCE

Marking the rotation of the seasons, a deciduous tree is constantly evolving, offering something new and beautiful to look at as each month passes. The first signs of spring are heralded by tiny veils of white flowers sprinkled over the bare stems of blackthorn (*Prunus spinosa*), which preface the more dramatic displays of cherry, magnolia, and apple blossoms that come later in the season. Lush green, purple, yellow, or variegated foliage follows to temper summer's heat, while fruit and berries start to form on many trees as the season ends. Fall then goes out with a bang as the leaves light up in blazing shades of red, orange, and yellow before falling to reveal the elegant sculptural silhouettes of trees throughout winter.

SPRING SPECTACLE

Many deciduous trees put on their most spectacular performance in spring, when buds burst open to reveal their flowers. While blossoming trees such as cherries (*Prunus* species), magnolias, and apples (*Malus* species) are among the most popular, catkins can be equally beautiful and often appear slightly earlier, providing a long season of interest if you can squeeze in both types of tree. For catkins, try the corkscrew hazel (*Corylus avellana* 'Contorta') and gray alder *Alnus incana* 'Aurea' in a small garden or opt for a birch (*Betula* species) in a larger space. The goat or pussy willow (*Salix caprea*) is especially prized for the furry oval catkins on the male plants in spring. While *Salix* are insect-pollinated, most male catkins, including those on the other plants named here, send clouds of pollen into the air, using wind to pollinate the female catkins or flowers, so you may want to choose a blossoming tree or goat willow if you suffer from allergies.

The catkins of the white-barked paper birch (*Betula papyrifera*) appear during the first days of spring.

The crab apple 'Liset' is covered with bright pink blossoms in mid-spring, followed by dark red, cherrylike fruit.

Fresh yellow leaves add a burst of summer color on the golden honey locust tree.

The dark foliage of the purple-leaved plum contrasts beautifully with bright green-leaved plants and colorful flowers.

Variegated leaves and white flowers decorate the tiered stems of the wedding cake tree throughout summer.

SUMMER FOLIAGE AND FRUITS

The foliage of trees is the main focus in summer, so if you use your yard mostly at this time of year, choose a tree with leaves that are colorful, textured, or interestingly shaped. The medium-sized golden honey locust *Gleditsia triacanthos* f. *inermis* 'Sunburst' is loved for its vibrant yellow young foliage, while the compact purple-leaved plum, *Prunus cerasifera* 'Nigra', has dark leaves that look especially beautiful when backlit in a sunny garden. The bright variegated foliage of *Acer negundo* 'Flamingo', with pink-edged green leaves, will also suit a small space.

A few trees flower in summer, too. The beautiful Japanese flowering dogwood, *Cornus kousa*, is one of the best examples; its leafy stems are covered with white or pink flower heads in early summer, followed later in the season with strawberry-like fruits. Another good choice is the wedding cake tree, *Cornus controversa* 'Variegata', which produces domed clusters of white flowers in early summer alongside its wide-spreading white and green variegated foliage. This eye-catching tree would be suitable for a medium-sized yard with space to accommodate its tiered stems.

Fruits also start to form in summer, with apples and pears swelling and coloring up at this time, although few are ready to eat just yet. The small red fruits of *Amelanchier laevis* appear among the foliage in summer, while cherry trees also bear fruit now, offering treats to both gardeners and birds.

Acer × freemanii 'Autumn Blaze' is a medium-sized tree with magnificent crimson foliage in autumn.

The rowan *Sorbus pseudohupehensis* 'Pink Pagoda' is a beautiful, compact tree with pink autumn berries, which appear before the foliage turns bright orange and red.

The huge leaves of the stag's horn sumach (*Rhus typhina*) turn from yellow to orange and red in the fall.

FALL FIRE

Just as the flower garden is preparing to take its winter rest, many deciduous trees come into their own, putting on a spectacular finale to the growing year and outshining many of the colorful blooms that have gone before. Among the very best for autumn hues are the Japanese maple (*Acer palmatum*) and the larger, even more dramatic freeman maple, *Acer × freemanii* 'Autumn Blaze', its crimson foliage standing out against the pale silvery-gray bark of its trunk and branches.

In smaller spaces, cultivars of the rowan, such as *Sorbus pseudohupehensis* 'Pink Pagoda', will liven up your yard at this time of year with their deeply cut, fiery foliage, matched with berries ranging in color from pink, orange, and red to yellow and white. Alternatively, try the more honeyed tones of a *Ginkgo biloba*—opt for 'Globosa' if you have a small yard. *Cotoneaster lacteus*, which is officially classed as a shrub but looks more like a small tree, will also brighten up your yard with its display of bright red berries, which appear among the semi-evergreen foliage and are loved by blackbirds. Another favorite for fall is the evergreen strawberry tree (*Arbutus unedo*), its strawberry-like fruits unusually appearing at the same time as the white urn-shaped flowers.

***Ginkgo biloba* 'Fairmount'** produces green leaves that turn a shimmering gold in the autumn before falling.

WINTER INTEREST

Trees have long been the focus of many midwinter festivals, supplying color and fresh foliage for the garden and home during the coldest, darkest season of the year. Hollies are among the favorite evergreens and come in a wide array of sizes, shapes, and leaf colors. However, if you want winter berries, choose a female form, such as *Ilex aquifolium* 'Handsworth New Silver' or 'Madame Briot', or the almost spine-free *Ilex × altaclerensis* 'Lawsoniana', because male holly trees do not produce fruit. Bay trees (*Laurus nobilis*) also offer winter leaf interest, and you can bring a few stems of a mature plant indoors to decorate the house, too.

Conifers come into their own in winter. Choose a dwarf or slow-growing type for a small garden, but check their final heights and spreads to ensure that they will fit your space because even those that grow slowly can get quite big over time. The slim sentinel pine (*Pinus sylvestris* Fastigiata Group) is a good choice—it grows quite tall but retains its skinny form. The golden-leaved yew *Taxus baccata* 'Standishii' and white cedar *Thuja occidentalis* 'Rheingold' also provide winter color and suit small yards.

Leaves are not the only source of interest in winter, and some deciduous trees more than match the evergreens. Those that have colorful bark (see *pp.102–103*), such as the Himalayan birch (*Betula utilis*) with its stunning ivory stems, or the shiny mahogany Tibetan cherry (*Prunus serrula*), will gleam in low winter sun. Others have rough-textured bark, such as the shaggy paperbark maple (*Acer griseum*). Some trees simply have a beautiful form that becomes more apparent in winter, such as the spiny hawthorn (*Crataegus*) or a fruit tree. These will sparkle when dusted with snow and frost, especially when silhouetted against a wintry sky.

A few trees flower in winter, too. The autumn cherry (*Prunus × subhirtella* 'Autumnalis') produces a smattering of tiny flowers throughout the cold months, while the cornelian cherry (*Cornus mas*) lights up a late winter garden with its sulfur-yellow blooms.

The golden evergreen foliage of *Thuja occidentalis* 'Rheingold' helps light up a small yard in winter.

Prunus × subhirtella **'Autumnalis Rosea'** produces a dusting of delicate pink flowers throughout the winter.

The intricate stems of a hawthorn create a sculptural feature when silhouetted against the winter sky.

USING TREES FOR PRIVACY AND SCREENING

Trees can help create a sheltered space in your yard where you can relax and entertain in privacy. Evergreen trees will provide a year-round green screen, while a deciduous species can offer a lighter canopy from spring to fall, when you are using the yard most frequently, while allowing more light in during the winter months. Choose your tree and place it carefully to ensure that it doesn't outgrow its allotted space because it will be very difficult to move once established (*see also pp.32–33*).

USING TREES TO CREATE PRIVACY

Of the many benefits trees offer, their ability to create privacy in the yard is at the top of the list for many people. A leafy canopy can mask the view from neighboring windows, while creating a cool, shady area below for dining and entertaining, but consider carefully the variety and size of your tree and where to place it for the best effect.

One solution is to plant a tree close to the boundary that adjoins the homes overlooking your yard, but this may require a very large specimen, especially if the properties are a few stories high, which may not be appropriate for a small area. Where space is at a premium, a more practical option would be to plant a smaller tree in the center of your plot or close to the area you want to screen. The diagram (*right*) shows how this works, and you can calculate the size you need by using a patio umbrella or similar prop to see just how tall your tree needs to be in order to veil neighboring windows.

Remember that a tree will cast shade, so before planting, check that it will not throw your whole yard into darkness (*see pp.32–33*).

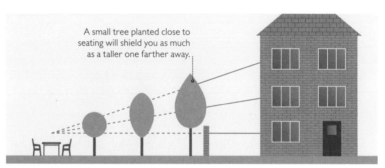

A small tree planted close to seating will shield you as much as a taller one farther away.

Trees of different heights can be used to shield a dining area from neighboring windows, but they will need to be taller closer to the boundary.

Multi-stemmed Himalayan birches provide privacy in this small city yard and will not grow as large as single-stemmed specimens.

Umbrella-pruned linden trees make a shady bower over this small seating area while also masking it from neighboring upstairs windows.

UMBRELLAS AND HEDGES

Training trees to contain their size and shape allows you to include larger species in a small space. For example, a linden tree pruned to create an umbrella shape offers shade and privacy on a patio, while interweaving a set of trees along a boundary will create a slim screen to mask neighboring buildings or eyesores. In the weaving procedure, the tree canopy is trimmed and trained on a box structure to form a narrow hedge on bare, stiltlike trunks, producing a geometric and effective screen that takes up little ground space. The best trees for intertwining include linden (*Tilia* spp.), beech (*Fagus sylvatica*), hornbeam (*Carpinus betulus*), and *Photinia* species. For most people, buying pretrained trees is the best option because it could take years to develop a hedge of the right size and shape for your garden. You can then call in an expert to trim the trees or learn how to do this yourself through online tutorials; both umbrellas and hedges will need annual care to maintain their shape.

A colorful apple tree disguises an old shed at the back of this suburban yard.

DISGUISING EYESORES

The canopy of a small tree such as a Japanese maple (*Acer palmatum*), fruit tree, or ornamental cherry (*Prunus*) will help disguise a shed or garage, drawing the eye to its blossoms, fruits, and leaves rather than the structure. For smaller eyesores, such as compost bins or trash cans, choose a tree with a short trunk and bushy canopy, such as a dwarf conifer or bay laurel (*Laurus nobilis*), or use a clipped yew hedge to create a screen.

CREATING WINDBREAKS

In windy sites, some trees can provide beautiful windbreaks to shelter you and prevent damage to the other plants in the garden. Trees with open canopies that allow some wind to filter through them are more effective than densely planted evergreens, such as a yew hedge, which could cause eddies on either side; taller conifers may also be more prone to blowing down in windy sites. If you have space, you could plant a double row of small trees, such as field maple (*Acer campestre*), Cornelian cherry (*Cornus mas*), or hawthorn (*Crataegus monogyna*). Alternatively, use a single line, planted fairly closely at 6½–13ft (2–4m) intervals, depending on the tree, combined with additional shelter from tough shrubs, such as sea buckthorn (*Hippophae rhamnoides*), hedgerow rose (*Rosa rugosa*), and *Elaeagnus*. Buy young trees, which will establish more easily in gusty sites than tall, mature specimens (see also pp.62–65 for more choices).

The hawthorn hedge at the back of this small yard has an open structure and makes an excellent windbreak.

HOMES FOR WILDLIFE

Few organisms do more to support biodiversity and wildlife than trees. Planting just one in your garden will deliver a host of benefits to fungi, bees, beetles, birds, reptiles, amphibians, and mammals, drawing them all into your plot to create a thriving ecosystem. While native trees may lure the most wildlife, all species that offer pollen-rich blossoms, a close network of branches for nesting and roosting, and fall berries or nuts will contribute to your garden's biodiversity and the health of the planet.

Birds such as waxwings flock to a *Sorbus* tree to feast on the ripe berries in late fall and winter.

HOW TREES SUPPORT BIODIVERSITY

Environmentalists often talk about how biodiversity plays a critical role in the health of the planet, and many gardeners are eager to do their part to help. The term "biodiversity" describes all the plants, fungi, animals, insects, and other living organisms that live in an area, and it is important because if anything is missing in that complex web, it can affect the whole food chain and cause an ecosystem to collapse. For example, some fungi help plant roots acquire food, insects eat plants, animals and birds eat insects, and other creatures at the top of the local food chain eat those animals and birds. Consequently, a lack of soil fungi will have a dramatic effect on everything else that depends on them.

Trees play a crucial part in supporting biodiversity, not only while they are alive but also when they die, feeding fungi, bacteria, and other microorganisms that decompose them. In Europe, some of the best trees for wildlife include birches (*Betula*), which support more than 500 species of invertebrate and many other forms of wildlife that feed on them, and oaks (*Quercus*), on which 280 different species of insect rely for forage and breeding. In the US, native cherries and plum trees (*Prunus* species) play host to a wealth of butterfly larvae and native bees, and willows (*Salix*) offer food for pollinating insects and grazing animals, such as elk (see also pp.112–115) To maximize the benefits to wildlife in your area, choose native trees or those that produce flowers and fruits to feed the insects, birds, and other creatures that live in and around your garden.

A silver birch tree, when mature, can support more than 500 species of insects, which provide food for birds and bats.

Small mammals such as voles will be attracted to fallen fruits in the fall to boost their energy stores before winter.

RICH STORES

As well as providing forage for insects, which hide in bark crevices and feed on both the wood and the leaves, trees also directly feed birds and small garden creatures. Finches, sparrows, and blue jays feast on the blossom buds of flowering trees. This can be annoying if you are hoping for a bumper fruit harvest later in the year, but by sharing your crop, you are helping keep these creatures alive when other food sources are scarce. Birds also enjoy the ripe fruits, berries, and nuts produced by many trees, while fallen fruits sustain insects as well as small mammals. You could also grow a hedge comprising different trees to supply a range of fruits (see pp.38–39).

PERFECT HOMES

Trees make safe homes for wildlife, offering cover from predators and protection during inclement weather. Birds use them as nesting sites and as lookout posts to spot danger; they also nestle in the branches to roost and sleep. Owls and other birds of prey roost and nest in the upper canopies of large, mature trees, out of harm's way, while smaller birds seek out prickly trees such as hawthorn and holly that provide a defense against predators, such as cats.

Pile up tree prunings on the soil in a quiet area of the garden to support insect decomposers and fungi.

THE VALUE OF DEAD WOOD

Many invertebrates feed on dead wood and help return its nutrient store to the soil, thereby sustaining plant growth and helping create new soil. Amazingly, in the UK, around 2,000 invertebrates are saproxylic, which means that they rely on dead or decaying wood for part or all of their life cycle. To encourage these soil-making creatures, leave some of your tree prunings in a quiet area of the garden for fungi, beetles, centipedes, and woodlice to feast on or use them as breeding sites. In turn, these tiny creatures will provide food for birds and bats and help maintain a healthy ecosystem in your garden.

Barn owls use large trees for nesting and roosting, so be wary of removing a mature tree in your garden that may be supporting them.

POSITIVE GROWTH

By planting a tree, you are not only creating a beautiful feature for your garden but also contributing to the health of the planet. These statuesque plants absorb and lock up carbon dioxide, a greenhouse gas that is partly responsible for climate change. They also shade hard surfaces, which tend to reflect heat and thus warm up the atmosphere, and some species even trap tiny airborne pollution particles. Planting trees stabilizes the soil and plays an important role in preventing floods, which are becoming a growing problem in our warming world.

Tree canopies help cool the air as water evaporates from their foliage.

Shading provided by trees cuts glare and cools an outdoor seating area.

COOLING THE AIR

No artificial screen will do the job of lowering high summer temperatures in your garden as efficiently as a tree. As well as blocking the sun's rays, a tree's foliage releases water drawn up from the roots via tiny holes in the leaves called stomata, cooling the air as the water evaporates. Siting a deciduous tree so that the canopy will shade the windows of your home in summer will reduce the need for air-conditioning, while one positioned close to a patio will provide a cooler, more comfortable space for relaxing and entertaining.

CARBON CAPTURE

Climate scientists predict that global temperatures are set to increase by 5.4–7.2°F (3–4°C) by 2100, principally as a result of the gases emitted by the burning of fossil fuels. The release of polluting carbon dioxide and other harmful gases is contributing to the phenomenon of global warming, which occurs when heat becomes trapped within the atmosphere. The solution to this problem is to cut gas emissions and to remove excess carbon dioxide from the atmosphere, and planting trees offers a simple and powerful means of doing the latter. All plants absorb carbon dioxide gas during the process of photosynthesis. The gas enters the leaves through the stomata, and in the presence of light and water, it's converted into sugars that sustain a plant's growth. In trees and shrubs, some sugar is converted into long-lived carbon-based chemicals that make up their woody stems. The carbon remains locked up in a tree's woody parts—often for hundreds of years—until it dies and decomposes or is burned. The bigger the tree, the more carbon it will store, so opt for the largest and longest-lived species you can fit into your yard for the maximum benefit.

Long-lived trees such as *Acer cappadocicum* are excellent carbon stores.

PROTECTING THE SOIL

Soil is naturally lost and stripped of nutrients by rain and wind, but the process is vastly accelerated when ground cover is removed and the land is used for intensive farming. Conversely, planting trees helps protect soils. By intercepting rainfall, trees reduce its power to remove nutrients. Their roots also bind soil particles, and their foliage diffuses the wind, minimizing erosion. Fall leaves enrich the soil with the nutrients released as they break down; invertebrates and microorganisms flourish as a result, improving water retention and the stability of the soil.

Leaves cover the soil with a protective blanket in the fall while feeding fungi, such as fly agaric. In turn, these help nourish tree roots.

TREES THAT ABSORB POLLUTION

Recent research has shown that tree and shrub leaves can fight pollution by trapping tiny airborne particles known as particulates. These particles pose a danger to human health, increasing the incidence of asthma, cancer, heart disease, and dementia. While all leaves trap some pollutants, studies show that those with hairy, rough, waxy, or scaly surfaces are the most effective. One study showed that silver birch (*Betula*) removed 79 percent of air pollutants, while yew (*Taxus*) and elder (*Sambucus*) both reduced pollution levels by 70 percent. Trees with complex leaves have also proved to be better traps than those with foliage that has a simple shape.

To benefit from their pollution-busting effects, plant trees close to boundaries that flank busy roads. For a hedge, use a mix of tree species, such as yew, hawthorn (*Crataegus*), and hornbeam (*Carpinus*), which research shows are especially effective against sooty black carbon emissions from vehicles.

Hairy leaves of trees, such as those of birch (above), *Cotoneaster*, and *Ribes*, trap air pollutants in their hairs.

Rough leaves, such as those of hawthorn (above) and hornbeam, trap particulates in the ridges and grooves.

Waxy leaves, including those of yew (above), holly (*Ilex*), and *Viburnum tinus,* make highly effective pollution guards.

Scaly leaves, found on many conifers including *Cupressus macrocarpa* (above), trap particles in tiny grooves.

Plant your tree where it can be seen from the house or a seating area, but not too close to buildings or boundaries.

PLANTING A TREE

Before buying a tree, check which soil type you have and how much sun your yard receives, and compare these conditions with the needs of your top choices to see which ones will be most suitable. Also, think carefully about where to position your tree, ensuring that the roots will not affect your property's foundations and that the canopy won't cast too much shade over your neighbors' yards. Then, give your tree the best start by following the planting techniques and tips shown in this chapter.

ESSENTIAL CHECKS

Trees cover almost every continent and are adapted to grow in a wide range of conditions, from the humid Amazon rainforest to the arid grasslands of the African savanna and even the freezing taiga close to the Arctic Circle. Although the environment in your neighborhood is probably more temperate, it is important to match the needs of the trees you choose with those your space can offer. Your local microclimate and the type of soil in your yard will affect the growing conditions, so make a few quick checks before buying to ensure that your trees will thrive there.

Birch trees are easy to grow, are happy in full sun or part shade, and will tolerate most types of soil, except wet.

Soil teeming with earthworms is a sign of fertile conditions.

SOIL BASICS

One of the most important checks to make before buying a tree is to test the soil in your yard. Soil is made up of sand, clay, and silt particles as well as organic matter, and the proportion

of each of these sediments in your soil, known as its texture, will determine its moisture and nutrient content. This, in turn, will also affect plant growth and the species that will thrive in your yard.

Sand particles are relatively large, and water drains quickly through the spaces between them, so a sandy soil will be free-draining and relatively infertile, because plant nutrients are soluble and also wash away when it rains. Clay particles are minute and trap moisture in the tiny gaps between them, which makes soils rich in clay dense and prone to waterlogging, but more fertile. Loams are soils that contain a good balance of sand, clay, and silt particles, allowing water and nutrients to be retained long enough for plant roots to absorb them, while excess moisture drains away, thereby preventing waterlogging. Loams are referred to as "moist but well-drained" soils in plant catalogs, on websites, and in the directories in this book.

Whatever the soil type in your garden, there will be a wide choice of trees adapted to thrive in it. However, in extreme conditions, where the soil is bone dry or very wet or unworkable, you can improve it by adding annual mulches of organic matter (see right).

CHECKING YOUR SOIL TYPE

To test your soil, dig up a small sample from just below the surface, leave it to dry a little if wet, and then roll it between your fingers.

Sandy soil feels gritty when rolled between the fingers. Generally pale in color, it falls apart when you try to mold it into a ball or sausage shape.

Clay soil feels smooth and dense. It retains its shape when molded into a sausage shape or ball, and a heavy clay soil can be bent to form a horseshoe shape.

THE ACID TEST

As well as assessing the texture of your soil, it is also important to check its pH value, which is a measure of acidity or alkalinity. Most trees will tolerate a range of conditions from slightly alkaline to slightly acidic, but a few prefer acidic soil, and their leaves may turn yellow if planted in alkaline types. To check the pH value of your soil, simply buy a testing kit from a garden center and follow the instructions carefully. In a large yard, assess the soil in different areas because it may not be uniform across your whole plot.

Soil pH-testing kits are easy to use and will give you results after just a few minutes.

Magnolias are best planted where they will not receive direct morning sun, which can damage the flowers after a frosty night.

SUNNY SIDE UP

When choosing and siting a tree, it's important to first assess the direction your yard faces and the level of sun it receives. Most trees enjoy a sunny or partly shaded site that receives a few hours of direct sun during the day from late spring to early fall. Very few trees thrive in deep shade, so avoid planting one next to a tall building or close to another large tree where no direct sun will reach it.

To check your yard aspect, stand with your back to the house and use a compass. A south-facing yard will receive light for many hours each day in summer, while a north-facing plot will be in shade for long periods, or all day, depending on its size and the surroundings. Try taking a few photographs of the space at different times of the day and throughout the seasons to help you map the sunny and shady spots. Remember, too, that once your tree is mature, it will itself create shade (see pp.32–33).

IMPROVING YOUR SOIL

The best way to improve the drainage of a heavy clay soil or to increase the moisture retention of a light sandy soil is to apply organic mulches. Spread a 2in (5cm) layer of organic material, such as well-rotted garden compost or manure from a reliable organic farm or stable, over the soil in the fall if you have clay or in the spring if you have sand. Leave a gap around existing trees and shrubs so that the moist compost will not rot their stems. Worms and other creatures will bring the organic matter down into the soil, where it will bind clay particles into larger aggregates, creating greater spaces between them for water to drain through. It also coats sand particles, enabling them to retain more moisture and plant nutrients.

Regular applications of organic material, such as homemade compost, will improve the structure of all soil types.

TOP TIP USE A THERMOMETER TO ASSESS THE MAXIMUM AND MINIMUM TEMPERATURES YOUR YARD EXPERIENCES THROUGHOUT THE YEAR AND ALSO LOOK AT THE OFFICIAL AVERAGES FOR YOUR AREA. THIS WILL GIVE YOU AN IDEA OF THE HARDINESS RATING YOU WILL NEED TO CONSIDER WHEN BUYING A NEW TREE.

CHOOSING A TREE

Buying a tree is an investment, in terms of not only its cost but also its value to the design of your yard and the wildlife that live within it. When choosing a tree for your plot, ensure that it will provide the benefits you are looking for by making a checklist of your needs. Then, contact a reputable nursery where staff will be able to provide guidance on the ages, sizes, and prices of the trees they offer.

Bare-root trees are sold from fall to early spring and should be planted soon after they arrive.

Select a tree that will suit your garden style and won't outgrow its allotted space after a few years.

FORM AND FUNCTION

Start your search for a new tree with a list of the functions you want it to perform, be that shade, privacy, flowers, fall color, or structure. Also, assess what style will best suit your yard design. For example, a hawthorn (*Crataegus*) would be perfect for a wildlife or Japanese-style garden but may not be the best choice for a family space, where the thorny stems could scratch children. Before buying, also check that your selected tree will thrive in the soil and levels of sunlight your garden receives (see pp.26–27).

SIZING UP THE MATTER

There are two factors to consider regarding tree sizes before you make your final purchase. The first is to check how big a tree will be after 10 years, 20 years, and when fully mature; most good tree nurseries will provide this information. These measurements will help you visualize the tree at different stages of its growth and ensure it has a long-term future in the space you have allocated for it, even if you subsequently move and never see it at its peak. A tree should stand the test of time and be an asset for those who will use the yard after you; a mature, decorative specimen can also be a selling point if you decide to move.

Some nurseries allow customers to pick out the specimens they want from the trees growing in their fields.

BARE-ROOT, ROOTBALLED, AND POT-GROWN TREES

When you are buying a tree, many nurseries will offer the option of bare-root, rootballed, or pot-grown plants. Bare-root trees have been grown in a nursery bed for a few years and are then dug out while dormant from late fall to early spring and sent to you with their roots wrapped in burlap or other material. Semi-mature deciduous trees and conifers may also be available as rootballed trees, which means they have been grown in an open bed, but their roots are contained in fabric, such as burlap. These trees are also available from fall to early spring but are more expensive than bare-root types because they tend to be older and have a well-developed fibrous root system that will establish quickly.

Pot-grown trees have been raised in the nursery in a container. They can be more expensive than the other options but are available all year and can be planted at any time, except when the ground is frozen or waterlogged.

This cherry tree was selected to provide a focal point in a lawn planted with spring bulbs.

BUYING A TREE

When purchasing a tree, as well as considering its aesthetic value, think about how much you want to pay for your new acquisition. Always buy from a reputable nursery, which may not be the cheapest but will guarantee that your tree has been either home-grown or imported with the correct paperwork to prevent the spread of pests and diseases. It will also ensure that the tree has been cared for properly, which will affect its long-term health. The price will be dependent on the age or girth of the tree and whether it is bare-rooted, rootballed, or pot-grown (see p.28).

Grown in pots, these semi-mature *Amelanchier* trees are expensive but will offer instant impact once planted.

TREE OPTIONS

When buying a tree, you will find that nurseries offer their trees at different stages of growth. The most commonly available are those listed here.

SEEDLINGS One-year-old seedling trees of vigorous species, such as beech (*Fagus sylvatica*) or yew (*Taxus baccata*), are available for hedging and planting en masse. They are usually sold by size, such as 2ft (60cm), and are a cheap option but will take many years to grow into full-size trees. Seedlings are a good choice if you are planting a hedge or a woodland garden and have the patience to wait for the trees to establish.

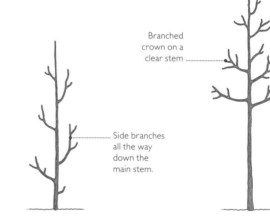

Side branches all the way down the main stem.

Branched crown on a clear stem

Feathered whips are three or four years old and have a few side branches.

Standard trees are older than whips and are measured by the girth of their trunks.

These small yew whips are inexpensive bare-rooted plants, ideal for planting closely to create a hedge.

WHIPS These two- to four-year-old trees have a central stem with little or no side branching and are normally sold by height. Often available as bare-root trees, they are inexpensive but will take a few years to mature into a garden-worthy specimen. One-year-old seedling trees with a single stem are also known as maiden whips; grafted bare-root fruit trees are often available in this form. A feathered whip is older and larger than a maiden and has side branches. Whips may need formative pruning to shape them (see pp.128–129).

STANDARD TREE If you're looking for instant impact, a standard tree will be your best choice. More expensive than a whip, these trees are sold by weight, rather than height, although most are at least 6½ft (2m) tall. They are measured by the girth of the trunk 3¼ft (1m) above the soil level, which is a good indicator of the age of a tree but not its final height—the dimensions are just the size of the tree when sold. Some trees, such as hollies and fruit trees, are available as half standards, with a clear stem of 4–5ft (1.2–1.5m).

ROOTSTOCK FRUIT TREE GUIDE

Fruit trees—and some other trees—are often grafted onto rootstocks that control their final height and vigor. Look carefully at the options available and select a dwarfing rootstock (*see right*) if you want a small tree that produces a good crop of fruit. Also, check whether your tree is self-fertile or needs a pollination partner, which means that you will require two trees for fruit to form. Some rootstocks provide other benefits, too, such as drought-tolerance, so ask your supplier about the site and soil conditions each tree requires as well as its size.

If you want a more vigorous tree, where fruiting may not develop until it is four or five years old, you can buy a specimen that is already that age and will fruit the year you plant it or the year after that.

This apple tree is grafted on a dwarfing M9 rootstock, which keeps it compact but still allows it to produce a good crop.

POPULAR ROOTSTOCKS FOR FRUIT TREES

This list shows the most popular rootstocks available for various fruit trees, although some suppliers offer a wider range. Staff at a reputable tree nursery will be able to offer you advice on which type will suit your particular needs.

APPLES

Rootstock: M27 (extremely dwarfing)
Suitable for: Small yards, containers
Starts fruiting: After 2 years
Height & spread: 4–6ft (1.2–1.8m) x 5ft (1.5m)

Rootstock: M9 (dwarfing)
Suitable for: Small yards, containers
Starts fruiting: After 2–3 years
Height & spread: 6–8ft (1.8–2.5m) x 9ft (2.7m)

Rootstock: M26 (dwarfing)
Suitable for: Small yards, containers
Starts fruiting: After 2–3 years
Height & spread: 8–10ft (2.5–3m) x 12ft (3.6m)

Rootstock: MM106 (semi-dwarfing)
Suitable for: Small and medium-sized yards
Starts fruiting: After 3–4 years
Height & spread: 10–13ft (3–4m) x 13ft (4m)

Rootstock: MM111 (vigorous)
Suitable for: small, medium-sized, and large yards
Starts fruiting: After 4–5 years
Height & spread: 13–15ft (4–4.5m) x 15ft (4.5m)

PEARS AND QUINCES

Rootstock: Quince C (dwarfing)
Suitable for: Small yards, containers
Starts fruiting: After 4 years
Height & spread: 8–10ft (2.5–3m) x 8ft (2.5m)

Rootstock: Quince A (semi-vigorous)
Suitable for: Small yards
Starts fruiting: After 4 years
Height & spread: 10–15ft (3–4.5m) x 10ft (3m)

PLUMS AND DAMSONS

Rootstock: Pixy (semi-dwarfing)
Suitable for: Small yards, containers
Starts fruiting: After 3–4 years
Height & spread: 6–8ft (1.8–2.5m) x 6ft (1.8m)

Rootstock: Torinel (semi-vigorous)
Suitable for: Small to medium-sized yards
Starts fruiting: After 3–4 years
Height & spread: 6–10ft (2.5–3m) x 8ft (2.5m)

Rootstock: Saint Julian A (semi-vigorous)
Suitable for: Small to medium-sized yards
Starts fruiting: After 3–4 years
Height & spread: 11–16ft (3.5–5m) x 11–13ft (3.5–4m)

CHERRIES

Rootstock: Gisela 5 (semi-dwarfing)
Suitable for: Small yards, containers
Starts fruiting: After 3–4 years
Height & spread: 6–8ft (1.8–2.5m) x 6ft (1.8m)

Rootstock: Colt (semi-vigorous)
Suitable for: Small to medium-sized yards
Starts fruiting: After 3–4 years
Height & spread: 11–15ft (3.5–5m) x 11–15ft (3.5–5m)

SITING A TREE

Checking that your tree will be in the best position in your yard is an important first step because it will be very difficult to move once planted. Make sure that the tree will provide shade where it is needed, such as over a seating or dining area in summer, and that it is not in the rain shadow of a building or boundary or too close to a hedge, where the soil will be very dry and it will struggle to establish. Always check local codes and neighborhood covenants when you wish to site a tree near a road or your property line.

This multi-stemmed Manchurian cherry (*Prunus maackii*) will cast dappled shade over the seating area.

MAKING AN IMPACT

When siting a tree, look for the area in your yard where it will have the greatest impact when viewed from either the house or another vantage point, such as a seating area. Try taking some photographs and drawing rough sketches of the mature tree on printouts to see how it will look in relation to the rest of the yard when in place. Remember also to check that your chosen spot provides the soil, sun, and space needed for the tree to thrive and develop its beautiful form.

Calculate where the tree will cast shade, too. For example, if you live in the northern hemisphere, placing your tree on the south side will throw more of your yard into shade than if you plant it on the north side, where it will block only the light beneath its canopy because the sun will never be behind it. An easy way to check where shade from a tree will fall is to place a patio umbrella in the intended position on a sunny day or to stand on a chair or ladder with a large umbrella and ask a friend to photograph the shady area it produces. Do this at different times so you can assess the light levels throughout the day.

The tree in this garden has been carefully placed so that it masks the building next door but does not interrupt the view of the countryside beyond.

KEEPING A DISTANCE

Take care when planting trees close to buildings because the roots can undermine the foundations if planted too close to a property. The root system of most mature trees is about equal to the width of the canopy, so a small tree that is 10ft (3m) wide can be safely planted 12–15ft (4–5m) from the house.

The soil next to walls and fences is often in a rain shadow and very dry, which will hinder the tree's growth if you plant too close to it. Also check that the canopy will not grow over a neighbor's yard; site it at a distance equal to about half the mature tree's width from the boundary. A tall boundary or mature tree nearby will also limit the sunlight reaching your plant, which may cause lopsided growth, so give your tree the light it needs to develop well.

Make sure the canopies of trees in front yards will not restrict access along a sidewalk or public path.

The roots of the young birch and other trees in this sloping garden are helping prevent soil erosion.

PLANTING ON A SLOPE

Trees planted on slopes have many benefits. As well as a tree adding color and texture to a hillside space, once its roots are mature, they will help prevent soil erosion after heavy rain.

A large tree will be more difficult to establish on a slope than a young whip (see p.30), whose roots will quickly adapt to the conditions to anchor it, while the immature canopy will put less strain on them in windy weather. After a few years, the tree will develop a broad network of roots that will secure it to the slope.

When selecting a tree for a slope, remember that even on a gentle incline, the soil will be well drained and nutrient-poor, so choose one that can cope with these conditions, and always stake it to keep it from blowing over while young. On steeper slopes, consider terracing the site to give your tree a flatter surface on which to establish.

The soil at the bottom of a slope will be wetter, and trees' roots will suffer if exposed to standing water for too long. Before planting in a valley, use other moisture-loving plants, such as ferns, to soak up the excess water, and plant the tree slightly above the soil surface. If the area is regularly waterlogged, it may be best to choose another site.

HOW TO PLANT A TREE

Trees will establish well if you plant them in a suitable site and soil (*see pp.26–27*) and keep them watered during dry spells until the root system is fully developed. The method here is for all trees, whether bare-root, root-balled, or container-grown. Make sure that you don't plant your tree too deeply, which can rot the stem; it should have a slight flare of stabilizing lateral roots at the base when mature.

Leave a gap around your new tree so that the roots are not competing for water and nutrients with other plants or grass.

The best time to plant a tree is late fall or winter, when it is dormant.

WHEN TO PLANT

Bare-root and root-balled trees are available only from late fall to early spring, and it's best to plant them as soon as possible after delivery—if the ground is frozen, plant temporarily in a large pot of soil or compost and delay planting in the garden until conditions improve. Never plant in waterlogged soil—if the intended site is often wet, choose a tree suited to these conditions, such as a river birch (*Betula nigra*) or *Salix cinerea*; site other trees in a drier location.

Container-grown trees can be planted at any time of the year, although they will establish well if planted during the same period. Avoid planting in summer, if possible, when the hot, dry weather will dry out the roots more quickly.

STAKE OUT

Most small trees or whips (*see p.30*) will not need a stake, and the push and pull of the wind will encourage the roots to grow. However, tall trees and those with a dense crown of leaves and small root ball will need staking. Use tree ties to secure the stake to the tree and check them every year or two, loosening them if need be. The roots should establish in two to three years, when the stake can be removed.

ANGLED STAKE There are a few ways to stake a tree, but an angled one will suit most specimens. Hammer in a stake at a 45° angle so that it meets the tree one-third of the way up the trunk, driving it at least 2ft (60cm) into the ground. Make sure that it is leaning into the prevailing wind direction.

UPRIGHT STAKE A good option for bare-root trees, a single upright stake should be one-third of the height of the tree, plus another 2ft (60cm) to hammer into the ground to keep it in place. Insert the stake vertically at the time of planting, on the side of the prevailing wind so that the tree is not blown against it. Make sure that it does not damage the roots and that there is a gap of at least 1in (2.5cm) between the stem and the stake.

DOUBLE STAKE This option is good for top-heavy trees, such as bay (*Laurus nobilis*), that are prone to snapping just below the crown, or large trees planted in windy sites that need extra support. Drive upright stakes into the ground on each side of the root ball and secure them to the trunk with two long tree ties.

Angled stake

Upright stake

Double stake

PLANTING METHOD

Follow these simple planting steps to ensure that your tree has the best start and establishes well in your garden.

YOU WILL NEED Bucket • Spade • Fork • Mycorrhizal fungi • Cane (optional) • Watering can or hose • Stake (for large trees) • Bark chips

1 Place your tree in a bucket of water for about an hour to soak the root ball. Meanwhile, dig a square hole three times as wide as the root ball and the same depth. Use a fork to loosen the soil around the sides of the hole. Apply some mycorrhizal fungi to the bottom of the hole to promote good root growth, but do not add any organic matter or compost, which may cause the tree to sink once planted.

2 Place the tree in the hole. Lay a cane or the spade across the hole to check that the point where the roots meet the stem will be level with, or slightly above, the soil surface once the tree is planted. Remove the tree from its pot and gently loosen the roots if they are coiled around the sides of the root ball. Set the tree in the hole.

3 Add a stake, if required. Refill around the tree with the excavated soil, checking again that it is at the correct level. Firm the soil to remove large air pockets, then water well. Apply a 2–3in (5–7.5cm) layer of bark chips over the soil, leaving a 4in (10cm) gap around the trunk.

4 Newly planted trees need to be watered regularly during dry spells for 2–3 years after planting. Once or twice a week, water the area by using a large can fitted with a rose head or a hose on a gentle setting, applying enough water for it to filter down to the roots at lower levels. This method mimics a rain shower and will sustain the tree's roots without dislodging the soil around them.

TOP TIP IF YOU HAVE HEAVY CLAY SOIL THAT IS PRONE TO PUDDLING AFTER RAINFALL, PLANT YOUR TREE WITH THE ROOT BALL SLIGHTLY ABOVE THE SURFACE, THEN COVER WITH SOIL, CREATING A SLIGHT MOUND THAT WATER WILL DRAIN OFF. THIS WILL KEEP MOISTURE AWAY FROM THE TRUNK AND REDUCE THE RISK OF IT ROTTING.

HOW TO PLANT A CORDON FRUIT TREE

Training a fruit tree as an espalier, fan, or cordon against a wall or fence is a great idea for a small garden. An espalier has a single trunk with horizontally trained limbs that form tiers of fruit-bearing stems, while the branches of a fan create a vase shape. One of the easiest options is a cordon, where trees grown on dwarfing rootstocks are trained at an angle, which encourages fruit to form on short side-shoots.

The stems of this fan-trained pear are trained on canes attached to wires, and it is pruned in the same way as a cordon.

STARTING POINT

Cordons are ideal for apple or pear trees that have been grafted on to dwarfing rootstocks (see p.31) and are spur-bearing, which means that they produce fruit on short side-shoots. Check these details carefully before buying and avoid tip-bearing cultivars that fruit on the ends of each stem because the fruit will be removed when you prune a cordon. Buy a whip that is one, two, or three years old (see p.30) from a reputable nursery, asking for advice on which cultivars would be best for your site and soil conditions.

The optimum time to plant a cordon is from late fall to late winter, when the trees are dormant and you can buy them as inexpensive bare-root specimens (see p.28). If your soil is very free-draining sand or heavy clay, improve it the spring before planting with a layer of organic mulch (see p.27), but do not add organic matter to the soil at the time of planting, which may cause the trees to sink and the stems to rot in the moist soil.

Choose a pear tree grafted on a Quince C rootstock to create a cordon against a wall or on wires attached to sturdy freestanding posts.

GROWING FRUIT TREES AS CORDONS

YOU WILL NEED Long bamboo canes • Tape measure • Strong galvanized wire • Straining eye bolts • Dwarf apple or pear trees • Tree ties or strong twine • Seasoned bark chips

1 To create a permanent support system, place bamboo canes at 28in (70cm) intervals along a wall or fence where you will be planting the trees. Then, attach three horizontal wires to the wall, ensuring that they are as long as your line of canes. Use straining eye bolts to fix the wires in place, so that they are 4in (10cm) or more away from the wall. Place the canes at a 45° angle and tie them to the wires.

2 Plant the trees adjacent to the canes but about 18in (45cm) away from the wall or fence, where the soil will not be as dry. Lean the stems toward the canes. Taking care not to bury the graft union (a scar or kink on the stem), cover the rest of the root ball with soil, cutting away any protruding roots.

3 Attach the trees to the canes by using tree ties or strong twine. Water the soil over the trees' roots and cover with a mulch of seasoned bark chips, leaving a gap around each of the stems. Cut back any side shoots that are longer than 4in (10cm) to three buds, leaving the main stem and any shorter side-shoots unpruned.

4 Remove the first year's blossoms in the spring after planting, which will encourage stronger root growth. Then, prune the trees annually as described (see *right*). Keep tying in the main stem (the leader) until it reaches the top of the canes.

> **TOP TIP** CHECK AND LOOSEN THE TIES ATTACHED TO YOUR CORDONS EVERY YEAR SO THAT THEY DO NOT CUT INTO THE BARK AND HARM THE TREES.

ANNUAL PRUNING

Prune your cordons in late summer. Cut back side-shoots more than 9in (23cm) long that grew from the main stem earlier in the summer to three leaves beyond the basal cluster, which is the group of leaves at the base of the stem (see pp.126–127 for pruning cuts advice). Prune stems that grew from existing side-shoots to just one leaf beyond the basal cluster.

Leave shoots that are less than 6–9in (15–23cm) long until early fall, then cut those back to one leaf beyond the basal cluster. At the same time, prune any new stems that formed after the initial summer pruning back to one leaf beyond the last cut you made.

When your cordons have reached the top of their supports, cut them back annually in late summer to maintain this length.

In late summer, prune the current season's stems back to three leaves above the basal cluster.

PLANTING TREES AS HEDGES

Hedges are essentially a line of trees or shrubs that are cut regularly to encourage dense growth and maintain a desired shape and size. As well as creating beautiful natural boundaries, they make excellent windbreaks in blustery sites and also offer habitats for wildlife. Hedges can range from compact to larger and more rambling features, so choose a style and plants that will suit your space and needs.

A trimmed yew hedge makes a beautiful boundary and offers a nesting site for small birds.

CHOOSING HEDGING TREES

As well as marking the boundary around a yard, hedges can be used to divide your space into different areas. Slow-growing evergreen trees, such as yew (*Taxus*) and holly (*Ilex*), provide year-round color and will take less effort to maintain than Leyland cypress (× *Cuprocyparis leylandii*) and other trees that grow very rapidly and require a few cuts each year to limit their size.

If your yard is exposed to strong winds, use a hedge made up of deciduous species, such as hornbeam (*Carpinus betulus*), hawthorn (*Crataegus*), and hazel (*Corylus avellana*). These plants allow air to flow through the hedge, which prevents eddies from forming on either side of it, and will provide better wind protection than denser evergreens. Install young plants, which will generally establish more easily than larger trees in blustery sites.

To create a wildlife hedge, use a mix of species that flower and fruit, with a few evergreens to offer winter protection. Prickly trees, including hawthorn and blackthorn (*Prunus spinosa*), offer birds safe breeding sites, while rowans (*Sorbus*) and crab apples (*Malus*) provide spring blossoms for pollinating insects and fall fruits to sustain a wide range of wildlife. Threading a wild rose through the trees adds another layer of prickly stems and forage for insects and birds.

Hedging made from hawthorn and other flowering trees creates a habitat beneficial for birds, including robins.

Hornbeam is a versatile deciduous hedging plant that is green in summer and retains its crisp, bronze, dead leaves over winter.

PLANTING A HEDGE

Follow these simple steps to plant a hedge using bare-root young trees, which are available from late fall to early spring. Yew is shown being planted here.

YOU WILL NEED String • Sticks • Spade • Ruler • Piece of wood or cardboard • Canes • Young bare-root trees • Seasoned bark chips

1 If the soil in your garden is very free-draining or heavy clay, apply a mulch of organic matter to the soil in the proposed site the year before planting a hedge. In the fall, tie a length of string to two sticks to mark where you plan to plant the trees. Dig a trench alongside it no deeper than the trees' root balls.
2 Using a ruler, mark the planting intervals on a piece of wood or cardboard—the spacing for most trees should be 18–24in (45–60cm) apart. Place canes across the trench to indicate the planting positions for the trees.
3 Plant each tree at the same depth as it grew previously, which will be shown by the dark area meeting the lighter area on the stem. Fill

in around the root balls with the excavated soil and firm it in with your foot to remove large air gaps.
4 Water the trees thoroughly. Add a mulch of seasoned bark chips,

keeping it well clear of the stems. Water the hedge for the next two years during dry spells until the roots are well established and the plants are growing strongly.

MAINTAINING A HEDGE

After planting a new hedge, cut back deciduous trees to 12in (30cm) and evergreens by one-third of their original height to encourage them to thicken up. In subsequent years, leave the top uncut until it reaches the height you want and clip the sides lightly, which will stimulate bushier lateral growth. If you are able to trim both sides, aim to create a flat-topped A shape, which will allow light to penetrate to the lower levels; if you have access to only one side, cut so that there is an outward slant from top to bottom. Never cut a hedge from early spring to late summer, when birds

may be nesting in it, and trim evergreens such as yew in early fall to prevent new growth from being damaged by frost.

A formal yew or beech hedge will need clipping once a year. When trimming a hedge for wildlife, take care that you do not remove all the blossoms: most trees flower and fruit on stems made the previous year, so cut a third of the stems in fall or winter each year after they have fruited, and then a different third the following year, and so on, noting which areas you have cut and when.

To prevent accidents, protect your eyes, ears, and hands when using an electric hedge trimmer.

UNDERPLANTING TREES

You can enhance the look of your tree by planting a medley of shade-tolerant shrubs, perennials, bulbs, and annual flowers beneath it. Choose plants that are suited to the conditions in the area where you plan to install them, checking the soil moisture levels and how much light the ground receives throughout the year. The conditions may differ within a very small space around a tree, where the canopy and roots will create a range of microclimates. Many woodland plants also make use of the extra light available in spring before the leaves unfurl and create deeper shade.

Astrantias, foxgloves, epimediums, dead-nettles, and geraniums create a colorful combination beneath a multi-stemmed deciduous tree.

WOODLAND WONDERS

Take a walk in your local woods or a tree-lined park, and you will see that a number of plant species thrive in the dappled shade beneath deciduous trees. Plants that are adapted to shade, which are known as woodlanders, include many beautiful bulbs that make use of the early spring sunshine that falls between the bare stems of a tree before the leaves unfurl as well as a collection of perennials and shrubs that are adapted to low light levels. However, almost no plants are able to grow beneath conifers, so bear this in mind if you want to plant one: the year-round deep shade they cast and the dense network of roots they form close to the surface produce hostile conditions for other species. Difficult growing conditions can also occur close to the trunks of mature deciduous trees, where the heavy shade and dry soil make it difficult for plants to survive, but the choice is wider for areas around the edge of the canopy, where more light and moisture are available.

Wood anemones appear in spring and, where happy, will naturalize and spread around an established tree.

CHOOSING SHADE PLANTS

Look for plants that can handle either deep or partial shade and choose a combination of shrubs, perennials, spring bulbs, and the handful of shade-tolerant bedding plants, such as impatiens

(*Impatiens*), tobacco plants (*Nicotiana*), and tender fuchsias to add some seasonal color. Shrubs such as *Daphne*, *Elaeagnus*, *Euonymus*, and *Mahonia* are good choices for the dappled shade at the edge of a tree's canopy, while perennials, including *Epimedium*, *Bergenia*, *Primula*, *Liriope*, *Pulmonaria*, *Geranium phaeum*, *Polemonium*, and *Alchemilla mollis*, will create a ruffle of leaves and flowers around them (see also pp.42–45 for more planting ideas).

Ferns such as *Dryopteris filix-mas* and *Asplenium scolopendrium* are tolerant of the deep shade and dry soil close to a tree trunk and add a lush leafy layer, while spring bulbs, including wood anemones (*Anemone nemorosa*), Spanish hyacinths (*Hyacinthoides non-scripta*), daffodils (*Narcissus*), and summer snowflakes (*Leucojum aestivum*), which in spite of its name flowers in early spring, will add seasonal color to these areas.

This group of shade lovers beneath a tree includes hostas, male ferns, *Iris siberica*, *Acanthus*, and *Polemonium*.

Mahonias grow well under deciduous trees, but leave sufficient space for their wide-spreading stems to develop.

PLANTING DISTANCES

Allow a newly planted tree to put down its own roots before creating an understory of other plants or, if you want an instant effect, leave a plant-free circle with a radius of 3¼ft (1m) around the tree. You can plant ferns and other deep shade lovers slightly closer to a mature tree, but buy young plants with immature root systems that can be squeezed easily in between the tree's roots. The competition from the tree may restrict the growth of these plants so that they never reach their potential heights and spreads.

You can improve the soil around a tree with annual mulches of organic matter (see p.123), but take care not to encroach on the area close to the trunk, as this will, in effect, bury it and increase the risk of it rotting.

TOP TIP WHERE A TREE'S ROOTS HAVE CREATED AN IMPENETRABLE LAYER BENEATH A TREE, DO NOT BE TEMPTED TO CUT THROUGH THEM TO ADD NEW PLANTS. INSTEAD, CREATE A RAISED BED OR USE LARGE CONTAINERS TO ACCOMMODATE YOUR PLANTING, MAKING SURE THAT THESE FEATURES DO NOT DAMAGE THE TREE'S ROOTS EITHER.

GRASS ROOTS

If you want a tree to decorate a lawn, make sure that the grass is 4ft (1.2m) away from the trunk after planting and while it is establishing. You can then sow a shade-tolerant lawn seed mix or lay sod up to about 18in (45cm) away from the trunk; this gap will help prevent damage to the tree when you mow the grass. Install your lawn in spring, so that it is not immediately covered with a layer of autumn leaves. In subsequent years, remove the fallen leaves with a flat-tined rake and spread them around your plants in beds and borders or make them into leaf mold by putting them into a plastic trash bag and leaving them to decompose for a year or two. You can then use the mold as a mulch.

Leave a gap around a tree to allow space for its roots to establish and to avoid damaging it when mowing.

UNDERSTORY PLANTS

This selection of plants that thrive in shade will help you blend your tree into the rest of the yard, while also creating an even richer habitat for wildlife. Select a few shrubs, perennials, and bulbs to produce a matrix of color and texture and follow the planting instructions on pp.40–41. Other suggestions include bergenias, primroses (*Primula vulgaris*), pulmonarias, cyclamens, and fringe cups (*Tellima grandiflora*), with their wands of fragrant yellow spring flowers. The shrubs euonymus, mahonia, and Japanese laurel (*Aucuba japonica*) also thrive in shade.

WOOD ANEMONE *ANEMONE NEMOROSA*

HEIGHT AND SPREAD 8 × 8in (20 × 20cm)
SOIL Moist but well-drained
HARDINESS Zones 4–9
SUN ☼

The diminutive wood anemone has deeply cut green leaves that form a ruffle around the round white flowers with yellow anthers that appear in spring. The rhizomes of this plant look like little twigs and are best planted in groups in the fall at a depth of about ¾in (2cm) and 3in (8cm) apart. Soak them before planting to speed up their growth. The plant dies back after flowering, so take care not to dig up the dormant rhizomes in summer when filling gaps in the border.

The dainty wood anemone will spread beneath a tree to form a carpet of spring flowers.

BEAR'S BREECHES *ACANTHUS MOLLIS*

HEIGHT AND SPREAD up to 5 × 3ft (1.5 × 0.9m)
SOIL Well-drained
HARDINESS Zones 7–10
SUN ☼ ☼

Grown for their huge, glossy, dark green lobed leaves, as well as the tall stems of striking hooded white and dusky purple flowers, bear's breeches bloom in late summer and make an eye-catching addition to a planting scheme beneath a tree. Although this large perennial plant offers a sculptural focal point, it will soon spread, so ensure that you have space for it before buying. It will flower best on the outer edges of a tree's canopy, where there is a little more light and moisture.

Bear's breeches are large, impressive plants with tall stems of hooded flowers in summer.

HART'S TONGUE FERN *ASPLENIUM SCOLOPENDRIUM*

HEIGHT AND SPREAD 24 × 24in (60 × 60cm)
SOIL Moist but well-drained
HARDINESS Zones 4–9
SUN ☼ ☀

This elegant fern is a compact evergreen that will make a neat rosette of wavy-edged leaves beneath a tree canopy. Tolerant of dry soil as well as shade, it will thrive close to the trunk, where it provides a ruffle of much-needed color in winter. Grow it alongside bulbs such as the wood anemone and wild daffodils (*Narcissus pseudonarcissus*) to create a colorful display in spring. Cut back old or ratty leaves in early spring to keep it looking neat and make way for new growth.

The hart's tongue fern produces a fountain of bright green wavy-edged leaves.

DAPHNE *DAPHNE*

HEIGHT AND SPREAD up to 12 × 5ft (4 × 1.5m)
SOIL Moist but well-drained
HARDINESS Zones 4–9 (depending on species)
SUN ☼ ☽

Celebrated for their sweetly scented winter or spring flowers and glossy evergreen or semi-evergreen leaves, daphnes are a great choice for a woodland area of the garden. Plant them on the edge of the canopy and check hardiness ratings if you live in a cold area because some, including the popular *D. bholua* 'Jacqueline Postill', may suffer in low temperatures. The hardier *D. × transatlantica* is a better choice for these sites and, unusually, produces flowers from spring to fall.

*Daphne ×
transatlantica*
'Eternal
Fragrance'
produces its
pink-flushed white
flowers from
spring to fall.

FOXGLOVE *DIGITALIS PURPUREA*

HEIGHT AND SPREAD up to 6 × 2ft (1.8 × 0.6m)
SOIL Moist but well-drained
HARDINESS Zones 4–9
SUN ☽

Often seen gracing shady borders close to trees, foxgloves provide a splash of color in summer when their elegant spires of tubular flowers appear. These biennials or short-lived perennials come in many colors, from white and apricot to pink and purple; although they may flower for only one season, where happy they will self-seed to provide a show in future years. They prefer dappled sunlight, so plant them at the edge of a tree canopy for the best blooms.

Foxgloves are commonly seen in woodland gardens and come in a wide range of jewel colors.

MALE FERN *DRYOPTERIS FILIX-MAS*

HEIGHT AND SPREAD 3¼ × 3¼ft (1 × 1m)
SOIL Well-drained/moist but well-drained
HARDINESS Zones 4–8
SUN ☼ ☀

One of the best ferns for the dry soil beneath a mature tree, the male fern resembles a giant shuttlecock when its sprays of large, triangular, feathery fronds appear in spring. The leaves will often overwinter in mild areas, but they then need to be cut back in late winter to make way for new growth, which looks beautiful as it unfurls. This temporary gap in a border also provides the space and light for spring bulbs to bloom. An organic mulch will help keep these handsome ferns thriving.

The male fern's shuttlecock of fronds makes a dramatic statement beneath a tree.

FRAGRANT OLIVE *ELAEAGNUS*

HEIGHT AND SPREAD up to 10 × 10ft (3 × 3m)
SOIL Well-drained/moist but well-drained
HARDINESS Zones 2–9 (depending upon species/cultivar)
SUN ☼ ☽

This tough shrub will be happy in the dappled light and dry soil beneath a deciduous tree. While some fragrant olives have silvery foliage better suited to sunny sites, the darker green *Elaeagnus × submacrophylla* is a good choice for shady areas —the cultivar 'Gilt Edge', which has green leaves with yellow margins, will shine out of the gloom. It also produces inconspicuous, scented, silvery flowers in summer. It is easy to care for once established; just prune wayward stems in spring.

'Gilt Edge' is one of the best fragrant olives for providing color in shady areas.

BARRENWORT *EPIMEDIUM*

HEIGHT AND SPREAD 12 × 12in (30 × 30cm)
SOIL Moist but well-drained
HARDINESS Zones 3–9
SUN ☀

Loved for its heart-shaped leaves and dainty nodding spring flowers, barrenwort is one of the easiest plants to grow beneath a tree. There are many species and cultivars, some with patterned or red-tinted leaves, and you can choose from flowers in shades of yellow, pink, purple, orange, and white. Simply cut back the old leaves in spring to reveal the blooms, which are often hidden beneath the foliage; the plant will then form a beautiful leafy carpet for the rest of the year.

Epimedium x warleyense has small bright coppery-orange and pale yellow flowers.

SNOWDROP *GALANTHUS*

HEIGHT AND SPREAD up to 8 × 2in (20 × 5cm)
SOIL Moist but well-drained, alkaline to neutral
HARDINESS Zones 3–8
SUN ☀

The timeless elegance of the snowdrop's white nodding flowers brings cheer to the late winter garden, the stems pushing through the soil unscathed despite the inhospitable conditions. There are hundreds of species and cultivars to choose from, some barely 4in (10cm) in height, others twice that size, each with green patterning on the petals. Buy them "in the green" (in leaf) in spring after the flowers have faded and plant in consistently moist soil—add a leaf-mold mulch around them in spring.

Galanthus 'S. Arnott' is an award-winning tall variety with nodding white flowers.

DUSKY CRANESBILL *GERANIUM PHAEUM*

HEIGHT AND SPREAD 24 × 36in (60 × 90cm)
SOIL Well-drained
HARDINESS Zones 3–7
SUN ☀ ☀ ☀

Many cranesbills can handle the shady conditions beneath a tree, but none is better than *Geranium phaeum*, which will also thrive in dry soil. The deeply lobed leaves are decorated with dark purple patterns and form a weed-suppressing carpet, while sprays of small, nodding, maroon flowers appear from late spring. Cultivars include the white-flowered 'Album' and 'Lily Lovell', which has bright purple blooms. Cut back the faded flowering stems for more blooms in midsummer.

The dusky cranesbill 'Samobor' offers dark maroon flowers and patterned foliage.

HELLEBORE *HELLEBORUS*

HEIGHT AND SPREAD up to 3¼ × 3¼ft (1 × 1m)
SOIL Moist but well-drained
HARDINESS Zones 6–9
SUN ☀ ☀ ☀

No shady border beneath a tree is complete without some hellebores. The round blooms of these versatile plants come in a wide range of colors, including pink, purple, red, white, yellow, and green; some also have marbled foliage. Most hellebores are about knee-height, with dark green or patterned evergreen leaves; old foliage can be removed as the flowers start to bloom. The popular *H. hybridus* is hardy, but a few of its cultivars are not and may need winter protection.

The Lenten rose, *Helleborus orientalis,* comes in many colors and blooms from late winter.

SUMMER SNOWFLAKE *LEUCOJUM AESTIVUM*

HEIGHT AND SPREAD 20 × 8in (50 × 20cm)
SOIL Moist but well-drained
HARDINESS Zones 4–8
SUN ☼ ☼

This beautiful, easy-care bulb masquerades under a very misleading common name because it does not flower in summer and is, in fact, one of the first bulbs to bloom in spring. It produces strappy leaves and tall stems topped with white, snowdroplike flowers with green tips that last for many weeks. It is sometimes listed as a sun lover but this, too, is not strictly true because it thrives beneath deciduous trees, blooming before they are in full leaf and then retreating underground in summer.

The summer snowflake will decorate the area under a tree in early spring.

BIG BLUE LILYTURF *LIRIOPE MUSCARI*

HEIGHT AND SPREAD 12 × 18in (30 × 45cm)
SOIL Moist but well-drained
HARDINESS Zones 5–10
SUN ☼ ☼

Big blue lilyturf may not be as large as its name suggests, but it is very useful for a shady spot under a tree, covering the ground with evergreen grasslike foliage for most of the year. In late summer or early fall, spikes of small violet-blue flowers appear between the leaves, adding color to the garden as the colder weather approaches. The blooms are then followed by black berries. Plant lilyturf in groups for the best effect, and it will then spread to fill any gaps between other woodlanders.

Big blue lilyturf is a pretty woodland plant with strappy foliage and violet-blue flowers.

DAFFODIL *NARCISSUS*

HEIGHT AND SPREAD up to 18 × 4in (45 × 10cm)
SOIL Well-drained
HARDINESS Zones 3–8
SUN ☼ ☼

From the classic yellow trumpet-shaped blooms to white flat-faced flowers, there is a daffodil for every garden style, but perhaps the best for dappled shade under a tree is the wild narcissus *N. pseudonarcissus*. Its dainty pale and darker yellow nodding flowers appear on short stems, and it will spread to form a carpet after a few years. Other dwarf varieties also lend themselves to these areas, so choose those that suit your scheme. Plant the bulbs in the fall; leave the foliage to die down naturally.

The dainty wild daffodil produces nodding pale and darker yellow blooms in spring.

JACOB'S LADDER *POLEMONIUM CAERULEUM*

HEIGHT AND SPREAD 36 × 12in (90 × 30cm)
SOIL Moist but well-drained
HARDINESS Zones 4–9
SUN ☼ ☼

The little green leaflets of this pretty perennial are arranged in opposite pairs and resemble a ladder— hence the name. In summer, clusters of small bell-shaped blue flowers with prominent yellow stamens appear on tall stems. This shade lover enjoys life at the edge of a tree canopy in dappled light, and removing the flower stems as soon as they fade will encourage a second flush later in the season. Jacob's ladder is a short-lived plant but may self-seed into areas that suit its needs.

Jacob's ladder produces tall stems of lavender-blue flowers with yellow stamens in summer.

The slim, flexible stems and small leaves of the tamarisk tree can handle salt-laden air and high winds, making it perfect for coastal areas.

TREES FOR DIFFERENT SITUATIONS

Whether your yard is flooded with sunshine all day in summer or shaded by nearby buildings, there is a wide choice of trees to suit your conditions. Tough trees that can tolerate salt-laden air or high winds in exposed sites may also be useful, helping provide shelter for you and your plants. The trees in this chapter provide choices for all these situations, and you will find more throughout the book—many thrive in sun or partial shade, although the choice is more limited for gardens in blustery areas.

JUNEBERRY 'BALLERINA' *AMELANCHIER × GRANDIFLORA* 'BALLERINA'

HEIGHT & SPREAD up to 20 × 13ft (6 × 4m)
SOIL Well-drained/moist but well-drained
HARDINESS Zones 4–9

SUN ☼ ☼
PRUNING TIME Winter
SHAPE 🮲

'Ballerina' is a relatively small variety of deciduous Juneberry that forms either a single-stemmed tree or a more shrublike multi-stemmed specimen; its branches spread farther outward as it ages. In spring it is covered with blossoms, each flower a delicate, pure white star shape, set off by the bronze-colored new foliage that emerges at the same time. The oval leaves are small, with finely toothed edges; they mature to green in summer and then take on striking orange, purple, and brown shades in autumn. The red-purple berries, which are produced in summer, are edible and also a good food source for many species of birds.

TREE CARE Ideally, plant 'Ballerina' in a moist, neutral to acidic soil, as it will not grow well in alkaline conditions (*see pp.26–27*). Water newly planted trees regularly while the roots establish in the soil. This tree will tolerate any aspect and exposure, relatively high air pollution, and full sun or partial or dappled shade. It is not necessary to prune Juneberry trees, except to remove any dead, broken, or diseased branches, but you can do some formative pruning on a young tree and take out any unwanted branches on an older tree to shape it if you wish. Carry out all pruning in winter while the tree is dormant.

'Ballerina' is a compact form of Juneberry with white star-shaped spring blossoms and red-purple fruits.

The leaf shape on the paper mulberry tree is variable, depending on the age of the foliage.

PAPER MULBERRY *BROUSSONETIA PAPYRIFERA*

HEIGHT & SPREAD 13 × 13ft (4 × 4m)
SOIL Well-drained/moist but well-drained
HARDINESS Zones 6–9

SUN ☼
PRUNING TIME Winter
SHAPE 🌳

The paper mulberry is so called because in Japan its bark was used to make paper. It is a deciduous tree that can produce suckering shoots from the base and therefore resembles a large shrub. The plants are either male or female. The former produce pale green and white hanging catkins, while the latter have rounded clusters of pink flowers in spring that, if pollinated, are followed by orange fruits. These are edible and quite sweet. You may not be able to source a particular sex of tree and will have to wait until it matures (10–15 years) to find out which yours is. The gray-green leaves are large, about 4in (20cm) long; they are divided into three lobes when young, maturing to an elongated, pointed oval shape. They are covered in soft hairs on both sides, with the underside distinctly soft and velvety to the touch.

TREE CARE Give the paper mulberry a sheltered, warm position in a south- or west-facing aspect because growth may be poor in a cold or exposed location. Water young trees regularly until they are established. Remove suckering shoots as they appear around the base, and prune in winter in the early years to create a balanced framework of branches in the crown. After that, the tree only needs any damaged, dead, or diseased branches removed.

INDIAN BEAN TREE *CATALPA BIGNONIOIDES*

HEIGHT & SPREAD up to 39 × 26ft (12 × 8m)
SOIL Well-drained/moist but well-drained
HARDINESS Zones 5–9

SUN ☼
PRUNING TIME Winter
SHAPE 🌳

The Indian bean tree is a spreading deciduous tree with a bushy crown. Although it can reach up to 12m (39ft), in temperate climates it is more likely to be around 6m (20ft) high after 50 years. Its leaves are large, light green, and heart-shaped; the foliage of the variety 'Aurea' is more golden in color. In summer, upright spikes of orchidlike white blooms with purple and orange speckles adorn the branches. These are high in particularly nutritious pollen and nectar, which are beneficial to pollinating insects. Slender bean pods follow them in late summer, each up to 18in (45cm) long, hanging in clusters that persist on the tree into winter after the leaves fall.

TREE CARE *Catalpa* is native to the southern US (the "Indian" part of its common name refers to the Indigenous tribe it is named for, the Catawba) and in temperate climates needs a sheltered, sunny position. Exposure to strong winds may shred the leaves, and frost can damage new shoots and emerging leaves. Newly planted trees will need regular watering while they establish. Once they are mature, the trees are low-maintenance; remove any dead, diseased, or damaged branches in winter. For larger leaves and to restrict the size, cut all the stems back to a clear trunk every year or two in late winter (known as pollarding).

The flowers on the Indian bean tree, held in upright spikes, resemble those of the horse chestnut tree.

In spring, the Judas tree bears a profusion of cotton-candy pink flowers set against bronze-tinted foliage.

JUDAS TREE *CERCIS SILIQUASTRUM*

HEIGHT & SPREAD 26 × 26ft (8 × 8m)
SOIL Well-drained
HARDINESS Zones 6–9

SUN ☼
PRUNING TIME Spring
SHAPE 🌳

The Judas tree is at its most spectacular in spring, when the branches are covered with pink flowers, but it is a beautiful deciduous tree for a sheltered yard at any time of year. The branches are spreading and bushy—without formative pruning, it will form a multi-stemmed tree. Plant it in a border with smaller plants beneath or as a specimen tree. It is slow-growing and not likely to be bigger than 13ft (4m) in height and spread after 20 years. The leaves emerge bronze-tinted in spring when the blossoms are still on the tree, then turn mid-green for summer and a strong golden-yellow in the fall. They are heart-shaped, giving the tree its other common name, the love tree. Meanwhile the flowers, which are popular with pollinators, transform into flat, beanlike seed pods around 5in (12cm) in length, green initially and then purple-brown in the fall and winter.

TREE CARE Plant in a sunny position; it will do best in a sheltered yard with a south- or west-facing aspect and well-drained soil. Water a newly planted tree regularly; once established, it will need little to no maintenance. Prune after it flowers, if needed, to remove damaged, dead, or diseased branches or to lightly shape it by taking out badly positioned branches.

The combination of the creamy-white leaf margins and red young stems of 'Variegata' creates an attractive effect.

WEDDING CAKE TREE *CORNUS CONTROVERSA* 'VARIEGATA'

HEIGHT & SPREAD 13 × 13ft (4 × 4m)
SOIL Well-drained/moist but well-drained
HARDINESS Zones 5–8

SUN ☼ ☼
PRUNING TIME Winter
SHAPE

Cornus controversa 'Variegata' is a small deciduous tree with branches held almost at right angles to the trunk in tiers, resembling the layers of a large cake (hence its common name). New shoots have a bright red tint, which fades to a burgundy shade on the older bark: combined with the branch structure, this makes it an interesting tree even in winter. The narrowly ovate leaves, green in the middle and creamy white at the margins, have a pointed tip. From a distance the tree in leaf appears almost entirely white or cream in color and is striking against a background of darker foliage. Flat clusters of tiny individual creamy flowers appear in summer, followed by dark purple, almost black, berrylike fruits. These are inedible for humans but popular with birds.

TREE CARE Although this tree will tolerate some shade, it will perform best in a sunny, sheltered spot. Ensure it is regularly watered in its first two years, while the roots establish; water mature trees only in a severe drought to prevent the leaves from scorching (turning brown). It needs no pruning other than to remove dead, damaged, or diseased branches, although you could also prune off any shoots on the lower trunk to keep a clear stem below the bottom tier of branches.

MAIDENHAIR TREE *GINKGO BILOBA*

HEIGHT & SPREAD up to 59 × 29ft (18 × 9m)
SOIL Well-drained
HARDINESS Zones 4–9

SUN ☼
PRUNING TIME Winter
SHAPE

Also known as the fossil tree, the maidenhair tree is one of the oldest tree species in the world, dating back more than 240 million years. While it can reach enormous heights, it is very slow-growing and makes a lovely upright specimen for a sunny spot. Younger trees can be columnar in shape, but their stems spread out more as they mature. The leaves are an unusual fan shape, sometimes split centrally into two lobes. Yellow-green in summer, in the fall they turn a bright, buttery yellow, and when they fall, they tend to do so all at once, over a day or so. The female trees have insignificant green flowers in spring that, if pollinated, are followed by spherical yellow fruits with an unpleasant scent. The variety 'Compacta' grows to only 13ft (4m) tall with a slightly wider, more spreading habit than the species.

TREE CARE Maidenhair trees need well-drained soil and a sunny position to do well, although they tolerate some exposure to winds. They cope well with air pollution, which makes them good for urban spaces. Water young trees as their roots establish. Mature trees will need little to no maintenance and no pruning at all unless branches are damaged, diseased, or have died; prune these off in winter while the tree is dormant.

The leaves of the *Ginkgo* tree, seen here in the fall, have traditional uses in medicinal herbal preparations.

PRIDE OF INDIA *KOELREUTERIA PANICULATA*

HEIGHT & SPREAD up to 26 × 26ft (8 × 8m)
SOIL Well-drained/moist but well-drained
HARDINESS Zones 6–9

SUN ☼
PRUNING TIME Winter
SHAPE 🌳

The delicate yellow flowers explain why this tree's other common name is golden rain tree.

Pride of India trees are an elegant sight in a yard, forming a pleasing rounded or spreading canopy of deciduous foliage. The full leaf, of around 18in (45cm), is composed of many opposite pairs of ovate to oblong leaflets with serrated edges. The leaves are pinkish-red when they emerge in spring, turning deep green in summer and then golden-yellow in the fall. The yellow flowers are held erect on tall panicles (slender, branched stems) in summer; although individual blooms are small, the tree produces them in profusion, creating a dramatic effect. The flowers are followed in the fall by ornamental heart-shaped seed pods, which hang from the branches in large clusters. The papery, bladderlike pods are initially yellow-green, then turn bronze-pink in color.

TREE CARE *Koelreuteria* can be slow to attain substantial growth, so patience after planting will be required. Although hardy, they prefer a sheltered position away from cold winds, especially in northern areas. Planting in full sun will ensure the best flowering and fall color. Newly planted trees need regular watering while they establish. Mature trees require no maintenance. Dead, damaged, and diseased branches can be pruned out in winter while the tree is dormant, if necessary.

CRAPE MYRTLE *LAGERSTROEMIA INDICA*

HEIGHT & SPREAD up to 13 × 13ft (4 × 4m)
SOIL Well-drained
HARDINESS Zones 7–10

SUN ☼
PRUNING TIME Winter
SHAPE 🌳

The crape myrtle is an upright small tree that grows quickly and will produce flowers even when young if conditions are warm enough. The deciduous ovate leaves emerge bronzed, maturing to a glossy dark green, and are around 3in (8cm) long. However, the flowers are the stars of the show, appearing in late summer and holding on into autumn. Dense, conical panicles of showy magenta-pink flowers are held at the ends of the branches, making it appear as if the whole tree is pink in a good year—it will flower well only if the summer has been sufficiently hot and sunny. The brown and gray peeling bark is an attractive feature in winter.

TREE CARE This tree is hardy only to 23°F (–5°C) and is best grown in well-drained soil and a very warm, sunny, and sheltered position. It will grow well in southern coastal or urban spaces. In colder, northern areas, consider planting it against a south-facing wall or in a sunny courtyard, or even growing it in a container that can be moved under cover for protection from frost in winter and early spring. When young, it may require formative pruning to create a treelike shape, but a mature specimen can be left to its own devices, apart from the removal of dead, damaged, or diseased stems in late winter.

The crape myrtle adds some pretty late-season color for the gardener and nectar for pollinators.

CRAB APPLE 'JOHN DOWNIE' *MALUS 'JOHN DOWNIE'*

HEIGHT & SPREAD 26 × 13ft (8 × 4m)
SOIL Well-drained/moist but well-drained
HARDINESS Zones 2–8

SUN ☼ ☀
PRUNING TIME Winter
SHAPE ▲

'John Downie' is a vigorous, upright crab apple tree with an egg-shaped crown on a clear trunk. It has three seasons of aesthetic interest and is an excellent choice for helping garden wildlife. In spring, pollinating insects benefit from the profusion of white blossoms that open from pink buds. The apples that follow are about 1½in (3cm) long, elongated in shape with skins in shades of red, orange, and yellow. They are edible but rather bitter so are best cooked or turned into jelly. However, left on the tree, they will be very popular with birds, which will eat them from the bare branches in late fall and early winter, while small mammals will appreciate those that fall to the ground. The leaves are mid-green and ovate, turning yellow in autumn.

TREE CARE Crab apples flower and fruit best in full sun and a sheltered spot away from cold winds and frost that might damage the spring blossom. Water young trees regularly in their first two years; mature trees may need watering in prolonged dry spells when flowering and fruiting. Formative pruning can help establish a good framework of branches for the crown and a clear trunk. Carry this out in winter, along with any pruning to remove dead, damaged, or diseased branches.

'John Downie' is a heavy-yielding crab apple tree, bearing its attractively colored fruit in the fall.

The glossy-skinned fruits of 'Red Sentinel' remain on the branches from the fall to early winter.

CRAB APPLE 'RED SENTINEL' *MALUS X ROBUSTA 'RED SENTINEL'*

HEIGHT & SPREAD 13 × 13ft (4 × 4m)
SOIL Well-drained/moist but well-drained
HARDINESS Zones 2–8

SUN ☼ ☀
PRUNING TIME Winter
SHAPE ▲ ☁

'Red Sentinel' is one of the most ornamental crab apple varieties, named for the scarlet fruits that persist on the tree into winter. Cherry-sized, spherical, and glossy-skinned, they are edible (try making crab apple jelly or roasting them slowly). Alternatively, leave them on the tree for aesthetic interest in the yard and for the birds, which will appreciate the winter food supply. The spring blossom is a boon for pollinators such as bees, which love the large, single, white flowers held in clusters on the branches as the leaves emerge. It's a deciduous tree, upright in its youth, becoming more spreading with age. The mid-green leaves turn a bronzed yellow in the fall.

TREE CARE 'Red Sentinel' tolerates air pollution well and will grow in most situations, although it flowers and fruits best in a sheltered and sunny spot. Crab apples are hardy enough to withstand cold winters, but avoid planting in a frost pocket, as freezing temperatures will damage the blossom. Newly planted trees need watering regularly while the roots are establishing. Create a balanced framework with some formative pruning; after that, crab apples need only minimal pruning in winter while the tree is dormant. Take out only broken, diseased, or dead branches and any that are crossing or badly placed.

COMMON MEDLAR *MESPILUS GERMANICA*

HEIGHT & SPREAD up to 20 × 20ft (6 × 6m)
SOIL Moist but well-drained
HARDINESS Zones 5–8

SUN ☼
PRUNING TIME Winter
SHAPE 🌳

Medlars are ornamental deciduous trees that also provide a crop of tasty fruits rarely seen in stores. The variety 'Nottingham' is a semi-weeping and spreading small tree; other varieties are more upright in habit and can be given formative pruning to create a balanced framework. The leaves are an elongated oblong shape, glossy and dark green, with deep ribbing; they turn golden-yellow and brown in the fall. The large white flowers in spring are followed in the fall by round brown fruits with a flat base; both flowers and fruit are around 2in (5cm) across. Pick the fruits before the first frost and leave them to ripen further inside until they are soft, after which they can be eaten raw or cooked; they taste like a cross between a tart cooking apple and a date.

TREE CARE Plant in a sheltered, sunny spot to avoid frost damage to the blossoms, which would reduce the harvest of fruit. Give young trees a regular supply of water while their roots are establishing, but water mature trees only during prolonged dry spells when they are flowering and fruiting. After some formative pruning, medlars need little to no further attention. Dead, damaged, diseased, and badly placed branches can be pruned in winter while the tree is dormant.

Low branches on medlar trees can become weighed down to the ground when they are in fruit.

Pick mulberries regularly, as they ripen over a long period in summer, giving a succession of sweet, juicy fruits.

BLACK MULBERRY *MORUS NIGRA*

HEIGHT & SPREAD up to 39 × 26ft (12 × 8m)
SOIL Moist but well-drained
HARDINESS Zones 5–9

SUN ☼
PRUNING TIME Winter/summer
SHAPE 🌳

The older mulberry trees get, the more gnarled and architectural they look. They are broad, spreading trees, although they can be pruned to restrict their size. The large, heart-shaped leaves are mid-green in summer and golden in autumn before they fall. The green flowers are insignificant but are produced en masse and therefore valuable for pollinators. Following these, the fruits begin to develop, ripening gradually rather than all at once, turning from green to white to red, then a deep purple-black. The fruits are too soft to farm commercially: growing your own is one of the few ways to get hold of these delicious summer treats.

TREE CARE Plant mulberry trees in a sunny position, sheltered from winds that could damage their blossoms and brittle older branches. They can also be trained as an espalier on a sunny south- or west-facing wall. Young trees will need watering in dry spells, but mature trees should manage without irrigation. After formative pruning to establish an open framework, mulberries will need pruning only a little in winter to remove any damaged, dead, diseased, or badly placed branches. The spreading branches of older freestanding trees may need the support of a forked stake. Prune espalier-trained trees in winter and summer.

The **bluish-green foliage** of 'Conica' can be used as a foil for other colors within the garden.

ALBERTA SPRUCE 'CONICA' *PICEA GLAUCA* VAR. *ALBERTIANA* 'CONICA'

HEIGHT & SPREAD up to 5 x 3ft (1.5 x 1m)
SOIL Moist but well-drained
HARDINESS Zones 3–8

SUN ☼
PRUNING TIME Pruning is not needed
SHAPE 🌲

This dwarf spruce tree has a neat, conical shape. It grows slowly and uniformly, only around 4in (10cm) each year; mature trees require virtually no maintenance. The dense, evergreen needles are a dark bluish-green, though the bright new growth in spring is almost lime green. Narrow, scaly, green cones may appear in the fall. Use 'Conica' to add winter structure and interest to a mixed border, where it will also act as a dark backdrop to bright flowers through summer. Alternatively, grow as a topiary specimen or plant in a large pot. Container-grown trees can even be brought inside temporarily in winter for festive decorations.

TREE CARE 'Conica' tolerates a range of soils but prefers a neutral to acid soil pH (see *pp.26–27*); if planting in a container, use acidic potting mix. Plant in a position facing south, east, or west in full sun; it tolerates exposure to winds and cold but not to dry soil, which can cause its needles to brown and drop. Water young trees regularly for at least the first two years while their roots establish and water mature trees in dry spells. Pruning is not needed, but to make a sharper cone shape, the foliage can be trimmed in both spring and summer with hedging shears. Shake snow off the branches so they are not bent out of shape or broken by the weight.

CHERRY 'ROYAL BURGUNDY' *PRUNUS* 'ROYAL BURGUNDY'

HEIGHT & SPREAD up to 26 x 13ft (8 x 4m)
SOIL Well-drained/moist but well-drained
HARDINESS Zones 4–9

SUN ☼
PRUNING TIME Summer
SHAPE 🌳🌳

'Royal Burgundy' is a beautiful addition to any type of yard. It is relatively vigorous, forming an upright shape at first, but the crown becomes more rounded as it matures. The cherry blossoms are held in clusters, the double flowers a deep pink, with layers of petals like frilly petticoats. They bloom in spring, later than many ornamental cherries, and just before or at the same time as the new leaves emerge. These are bronzed at first, maturing to deep purple for late spring and summer, then turning a brilliant scarlet in the fall. The bark is ornamental, too, with a slightly bronzed tone and some peeling, providing winter interest. Plant as a

stand-alone specimen, preferably with clear sky or a lighter background from your main point of view, so as to best enjoy the dark foliage.

TREE CARE Plant in a sunny and ideally relatively sheltered position for optimum flowering and fall color. It grows well in most soils. Water young trees regularly for at least two years after planting while their roots establish, especially during dry spells. Prune only if needed, removing dead, diseased, damaged, or misplaced branches and keeping a balanced framework. Pruning in summer lowers the risk of silver leaf and other diseases to which cherry trees are prone.

The **cotton-candy pink flowers** of 'Royal Burgundy' are offset beautifully by the wine-colored foliage.

The white cylindrical flower heads of the bird cherry appear from mid- to late spring.

BIRD CHERRY *PRUNUS PADUS*

HEIGHT & SPREAD up to 49 × 20ft (15 × 6m)
SOIL Well-drained/moist but well-drained
HARDINESS Zones 4–9
SUN ☼
PRUNING TIME Summer
SHAPE 🌳

The bird cherry is a very large, spreading, deciduous tree, but worth planting if you have the space, especially for its value to wildlife. The variety 'Albertii' is more compact and upright and a better choice for smaller gardens. The blossoms open in mid- to late spring, the flowers around ½in (1cm) across, white with five petals, held on short spikes. They have a delicious almond scent and are rich in nectar, attracting many pollinating insects. The small, black, bitter cherries follow in late summer, sometimes into early fall, and are popular with birds and small mammals, although unpalatable for people. The leaves are ovate with a pointed tip and serrated edges, green in summer, then turning a bronzed yellow in the fall. Note that the foliage is toxic to livestock, especially goats.

TREE CARE Plant bird cherries in any soil except those prone to waterlogging. They flower best in full sun but tolerate a little shade and some exposure to wind and cold. Water young trees regularly in their first two or three years. Prune out dead, diseased, damaged, or misplaced branches to keep a healthy and balanced framework, but remove only what is necessary. Pruning in summer when there are fewer fungal spores in the air lowers the risk of the tree contracting silver leaf disease.

CHUSAN PALM *TRACHYCARPUS FORTUNEI*

HEIGHT & SPREAD up to 49 × 8ft (15 × 2.5m)
SOIL Well-drained
HARDINESS Zones 7–10
SUN ☼
PRUNING TIME Pruning is not needed
SHAPE 🌴

The Chusan palm is the hardiest of all palm trees and a good choice for yards in dry, drought-prone, or coastal areas. It grows slowly, spreading outward before starting to grow upward, reaching its ultimate height only after many decades. The evergreen leaves are large, up to 3¼ft (1m) across, held on a long stalk that connects them directly to the trunk. They are dark green and fan-shaped, with ridges radiating from the stalk to the leaf edges, where they separate on older leaves into a narrow and pointed fringe. The trunk is covered in fibrous, tufty hairs around the hardened old leaf sheaths. Trees are either male or female; yellow flowers are borne in large sprays in summer, and, if pollinated, they are followed on females by clusters of small, black, spherical fruits.

TREE CARE Plant in a sheltered spot in full sun, protected from cold winds and frost pockets. Strong winds can rip the leaves, giving a tattered appearance. It is hardy to around 14°F (–10°C) but will not tolerate winter cold if the roots are waterlogged. Trees can be wrapped in layers of protective insulation (burlap sacking, horticultural fleece, or similar) if extreme cold and wet weather is forecast. No maintenance is needed after initial watering while the roots of newly planted trees establish.

The Chusan palm is ideal for adding height to an exotic border in a sunny, sheltered yard.

JAPANESE MAPLE 'SEIRYŪ' *ACER PALMATUM* 'SEIRYŪ'

HEIGHT & SPREAD 8 × 8ft (2.5 × 2.5m)
SOIL Moist but well-drained
HARDINESS Zones 5–8

SUN ☼ ☼
PRUNING TIME Winter
SHAPE 🌳

'Seiryū' is one of the group of Japanese maples with leaves so finely dissected, they are almost lacelike. This variety is more upright than most but is frequently sold as a multi-stemmed specimen, which lends it a vase shape. It is medium-sized and slow-growing, so it can also be planted in a large container. Place among plants with dark-colored foliage or in front of a dark wall or fence to best appreciate the hues of the leaves. In spring, they emerge lime green, with a narrow pink border around the edge; they mature to a pale green in summer with red tips and edges, and in autumn turn shades of red and orange. The leaf color is best when the tree is grown in some shade, which will also prevent leaf scorch. Insignificant red flowers are borne in spring.

TREE CARE Plant in partial or dappled shade with plenty of shelter to protect the leaves from scorching sun and winds. Japanese maples will grow well in most soils but prefer a neutral to slightly acidic pH (see pp.26–27). Water young trees regularly while they are establishing and mature trees during dry spells, as dry soil can cause the leaves to become brown and crisp around the edges. The only necessary pruning is to remove any dead, diseased, or damaged shoots when the tree is dormant in winter.

The finely dissected leaves of 'Seiryū' take on blazing red and orange colors in the fall.

The Juneberry makes an autumnal focal point of brilliant color that lights up shady areas in the yard.

JUNEBERRY *AMELANCHIER CANADENSIS*

HEIGHT & SPREAD up to 26 × 13ft (8 × 4m)
SOIL Moist but well-drained
HARDINESS Zones 4–9

SUN ☼ ☼
PRUNING TIME Winter
SHAPE 🌳

The Juneberry forms an upright small tree or multi-stemmed large shrub that does well with exposed sites and can be used to provide shelter and screening close to a boundary. The ornamental gray bark of this deciduous tree creates a beautiful feature, especially when it is exposed in winter. The small, ovate foliage is bronze when it unfurls in spring while the tree is flowering, then turns a fresh green for summer. In autumn, the leaves are brilliant shades of red and orange. The profuse spring blossoms are made up of small, star-shaped, white flowers. Berries follow, ripening purple-black in summer; they are edible, but you may want to leave them on the tree for the benefit of birds. The berries and blossoms make the Juneberry excellent for wildlife.

TREE CARE This tree will grow well in most soils but prefers neutral to acidic conditions and dislikes alkaline (limy) soil (see pp.26–27). It will tolerate exposure to cold winds and full sun or partial shade. Young trees will need watering regularly until their roots are established. Remove suckers and carry out formative pruning in winter to maintain a single-stemmed tree, also removing any dead, broken, diseased, or crossing branches if necessary. Apart from this, little maintenance is required.

BLACK BIRCH *BETULA NIGRA*

HEIGHT & SPREAD 33 × 13ft (10 × 4m)
SOIL Well-drained/moist but well-drained
HARDINESS Zones 4–9

SUN ☼ ☼
PRUNING TIME Winter
SHAPE

Birches are relatively short-lived deciduous trees, and as a result they grow quickly. The black birch has an upright habit; to make the most of its ornamental bark, you could buy a multi-stemmed specimen, which will create eye-catching impact in the garden. Also known as the river birch, it is a very tolerant tree, growing well in poor and dry soils and handling waterlogged soil over winter, urban air pollution, and periods of drought too. The leaves are glossy, dark green in spring and summer and bright yellow in autumn; they are small and ovate, with a serrated edge and distinct ribbing along the veins. The bark peels and ruffles in attractive shades of rust, cinnamon, amber, coral pink, and gray. The tree also produces yellow-brown catkins in spring.

TREE CARE Black birch can be planted in virtually any soil and position in the garden. Water a newly planted tree regularly for the first two years until the roots have had time to spread out into the ground, particularly if you are growing one on poor or very dry soil. Black birch does not need any regular pruning except to remove any damaged, dead, or diseased branches, which should be done in winter when it is dormant.

The peeling, papery bark in a range of colors is a distinguishing feature of the black birch.

SILVER BIRCH *BETULA PENDULA*

HEIGHT & SPREAD 39 × 26ft (12 × 8m)
SOIL Well-drained/moist but well-drained
HARDINESS Zones 2–7

SUN ☼ ☼
PRUNING TIME Winter
SHAPE

The silver birch is a deciduous tree with a slender, elegant, upright growth habit and graceful weeping stems that will sway gently in the breeze. The glossy leaves are roughly triangular with serrated edges, mid- to dark green in summer and yellow in autumn. In spring, male and female catkins are produced on the same tree: the male catkins are long, pendulous, and yellow, the female ones shorter, upright, and green, ripening to burgundy before releasing their tiny seeds. The distinctive white bark becomes marked with dark horizontal bands and cracks as the tree matures. This is an excellent tree for wildlife, playing host to birds and hundreds of insect species. The variety *Betula pendula* subsp. *pendula* 'Fastigiata Joes' is only around 16ft (5m) tall, with a compact, pyramidal habit.

TREE CARE Silver birch can be planted in a wide range of soils and sites. Water newly planted trees while their roots establish. Mature trees need little care except for pruning out dead or damaged branches, which can be done in winter. Larger pieces of old bark that are hanging off the trunk can be removed and the trunk washed with very dilute soapy water to brighten it up again. Do not be tempted to peel bark from the stems to reveal brighter layers beneath, as this can seriously damage the tree.

Silver birch trees give a particularly pleasing effect when they are planted together in groups.

The dense, dark green foliage of the incense cedar is made up of tiny overlapping scales.

INCENSE CEDAR *CALOCEDRUS DECURRENS*

HEIGHT & SPREAD up to 82 × 20ft (25 × 6m)
SOIL Well-drained
HARDINESS Zones 5–8

SUN ☼ ☼
PRUNING TIME Pruning is not needed
SHAPE 🌲

The incense cedar, also known as the white cedar, is a long-lived evergreen conifer—wild specimens more than a thousand years old have been found. Very tall but narrow, in colder climates it forms a columnar shape, while in warmer areas it is more conical. The glossy, dark green foliage is made up of overlapping scales and held in flattened, fan-shaped sprays on the densely packed branches. When crushed, the leaves give off an aromatic, incenselike fragrance; hence the name. The bark is also aromatic; it is a rusty reddish-brown color and has a flaky texture, breaking off in sheets on older trees. Cones are occasionally produced—both male and female cones appear on the same tree, but on different branches. They are characteristically hooked at the top. Once ripe, they are not held on the branches for long.

TREE CARE Incense cedars are very low-maintenance trees, requiring no pruning at all. They do well in cold sites, but planting out of strong winds is advisable. Water a newly planted tree while the roots establish. Shake heavy snowfall off the branches where it's possible to reach them (use a rake or broom if needed), as the weight can cause their branches to bend out of shape or break.

JAPANESE CEDAR 'ELEGANS COMPACTA' *CRYPTOMERIA JAPONICA* 'ELEGANS COMPACTA'

HEIGHT & SPREAD up to 8 × 5ft (2.5 × 1.5m)
SOIL Moist but well-drained
HARDINESS Zones 5–8

SUN ☼ ☼
PRUNING TIME Pruning is not needed
SHAPE 🌳

'Elegans Compacta' is a smaller version of the Japanese cedar that suits a site in dappled or partial shade. It is bushy, with no strong central leader (shoot), giving it a roughly pyramidal shape that can become more spreading. As it is relatively slow-growing, it can also be planted in a large container. The long, needlelike evergreen leaves look spiky but are actually soft to the touch, making this an extremely tactile tree. They are arranged in spirals, giving each branchlet a featherlike appearance, drooping at the tip. Bright or mid-green in color in spring and summer, the foliage takes on a bronze tint in autumn, turning purple in the colder temperatures of winter. The bark is an attractive amber-brown color, though it is mostly hidden by the foliage.

TREE CARE This tree prefers a moist but well-drained soil and grows well in partial or dappled shade. Water young trees while the roots are establishing; water container-grown trees regularly. Pruning is not necessary, but remove damaged or dead branches in mid-spring to avoid frost damage to subsequent new growth. Heavy snow on branches can cause them to bend outward, compromising the overall shape of the tree, or they may even break, so shake snow off the tree as soon as possible.

The evergreen foliage of the Japanese cedar changes color in winter from green to bronze and purple.

HOLLY 'J. C. VAN TOL' _ILEX AQUIFOLIUM_ 'J. C. VAN TOL'

HEIGHT & SPREAD 20 × 8ft (6 × 2.5m)
SOIL Well-drained/moist but well-drained
HARDINESS Zones 5–9

SUN ☼ ☼
PRUNING TIME Spring/summer/winter
SHAPE 🌳

Holly berries are mildly toxic to people but are a good source of food for birds over the fall and winter months.

'J. C. van Tol' is a self-pollinating female holly tree, known for its profuse and reliable displays of scarlet berries in the fall and winter. The flowers that precede them are popular with pollinators; small and white, they bloom in spring and early summer, after which the berries form, bright green at first. The evergreen foliage is largely smooth-edged rather than prickly: the leaves are ovate with a sharp point, glossy, dark green, and leathery, borne on shoots that are dark purple when young. Grown as a single tree, 'J. C. van Tol' has a broadly upright shape, but it can also be clipped into a globe or other formal shape, perhaps on the top of a clear trunk to highlight the attractive smooth gray bark. Multiple trees can be used to create a dense hedge.

TREE CARE Holly trees grow well in dappled or partial shade and in any aspect; they do well in windy sites and all soil types, other than wet. Water newly planted trees while they are establishing. Prune freestanding trees as necessary to shape the framework and to remove dead, diseased, or damaged branches. Topiary trees can be clipped into shape in summer; trim hedges in early spring before the birds start to nest. Holly trees respond well to hard pruning to reduce their size if required.

TULIP TREE _LIRIODENDRON TULIPIFERA_

HEIGHT & SPREAD up to 39 × 20ft (12 × 6m)
SOIL Well-drained/moist but well-drained
HARDINESS Zones 4–9

SUN ☼ ☼
PRUNING TIME Winter
SHAPE 🌳

The tulip tree is a large, majestic specimen with an attractive crown of lush deciduous foliage. The glossy leaves are an unusual squarish, four-tipped shape about 6in (15cm) wide, with blunted lobes and a pale central midrib. They open a fresh apple green in spring, darkening in summer and turning brilliant yellow and gold in the fall. Once the tree is sufficiently mature (usually about 15–20 years old), it starts to produce flowers each summer. These are shaped like tulips, hence the name; lemony green with pale orange centers, they look like little bowls on the branches. They are produced throughout the summer, extending the period of interest for both gardeners and pollinators such as bees. They are followed by upright clusters of seedheads that resemble cones.

TREE CARE Tulip trees prefer a neutral or slightly acidic soil (see pp.26–27) and grow best in free-draining conditions. Those in full sun will grow slowly and have a more rounded crown than those in partial shade, which tend to grow faster and in a more columnar shape. They can handle some exposure to winds. Water young trees while their roots are establishing. Older trees should need little maintenance; prune damaged or dead branches in winter while the tree is dormant.

The unusual bowl-shaped flowers of the tulip tree are up to 2in (5cm) wide and sit upright on the branches.

YULAN *MAGNOLIA DENUDATA*

HEIGHT & SPREAD 30 x 30ft (9 x 9m)
SOIL Well-drained/moist but well-drained
HARDINESS Zones 5–9

SUN ☼ ☼
PRUNING TIME Midsummer to early fall
SHAPE 🌳

The yulan magnolia is an elegant, very slow-growing deciduous tree suited to planting in a woodland setting or as an architectural specimen in a cottage or urban yard. It can be grown either on a single trunk or as a multi-stemmed tree. Its fragrant flowers open before the leaves are fully unfurled; the blooms are slender, around 3in (8cm) long, and cup-shaped, rather like lilies. The white petals have a blush-pink base; they are held upright at first, then gradually open more widely. Mature trees can be covered in blooms, offering a magnificent sight in spring and early nectar for insects. The smooth-edged, ovate leaves unfurl initially an acid green, then mature to mid-green in summer. There is no significant display of fall color.

TREE CARE Magnolias need a position protected from harsh winds, the worst of winter cold, and frosts that damage the spring blossom. The yulan prefers neutral or acidic soil (see *pp.26–27*). Prune between midsummer and early fall if required, removing dead, diseased, or damaged wood. Carry out size reduction or thinning of the branches on an older tree over a few years to avoid causing the tree undue stress. Water young trees regularly, especially in dry spells, as the roots establish.

The flowers of the yulan magnolia unfold in spring, offering a wonderful lemon scent in the garden.

DECIDUOUS CAMELLIA KOREANA GROUP *STEWARTIA PSEUDOCAMELLIA* KOREANA GROUP

The Koreana Group of deciduous camellias display wonderful fall colors of red and orange.

HEIGHT & SPREAD up to 39 x 20ft (12 x 6m)
SOIL Moist but well-drained
HARDINESS Zones 5–8

SUN ☼ ☼
PRUNING TIME Winter
SHAPE 🌲

The deciduous camellia is an ideal small or medium-sized tree for a shady spot. Extremely slow-growing, it forms a roughly pyramidal crown, although it can also be grown as a multi-stemmed tree; the latter approach maximizes the appeal of the mottled, flaking, gray and brown ornamental bark. The cooler the climate, the smaller its ultimate size. The leaves are ovate with distinct veins, a slight curl to the edges, and a pointed tip; mid-green in summer, in the fall they turn to fiery shades of red and orange. The flowers are borne in midsummer but can persist until late summer in good conditions. Large and bowl-shaped, they have white petals and prominent yellow centers. They are followed by attractive segmented brown seed capsules with pointed tips.

TREE CARE Plant deciduous camellias in a sheltered location away from cold winds: they will thrive in partial shade and a moist acidic soil (see *pp.26–27*). East- or west-facing spots are best if possible. Water newly planted trees for at least two years during dry weather while their roots establish in the soil. Remove damaged, dead, and diseased branches in winter while the tree is dormant. Formative pruning and light pruning to shape the framework can also be carried out in winter if required.

JAPANESE SNOWBELL *STYRAX JAPONICUS* 'FARGESII'

HEIGHT & SPREAD up to 33 × 20ft (10 × 6m)
SOIL Moist but well-drained
HARDINESS Zones 6–8

SUN ☀ ☀
PRUNING TIME Winter/summer
SHAPE 🌳

'Fargesii' is a beautiful cultivar with larger leaves and flowers than the species; it is also considered to be more robust. While most trees bloom in spring, the Japanese snowbell is prized for its summer flowers. It has an arching, fan-shaped crown of glossy, deciduous foliage; the smooth leaves are light to mid-green, oblong with slightly serrated edges. In the fall they turn yellow and orange. 'Fargesii' blooms in early to midsummer, with the flowers hanging from the underside of the branches. About 1in (2.5cm) across, they are bell-shaped, with fused, pointed, white petals that curve upward at their tips and yellow stamens. They are also scented and popular with pollinating insects. Small, green, inedible, globular fruits follow the flowers.

TREE CARE A woodland-style setting is ideal for 'Fargesii', but it will thrive anywhere protected from cold winds. It prefers a well-drained but rich, moist soil, neutral or slightly acidic (see pp.26–27), in partial shade or full sun. Prune in winter to remove dead, damaged, or diseased branches. No other pruning is needed except to restrict the size if wanted. It can also be pruned in summer after flowering. Water a young tree while its roots establish; mature trees should not need watering if planted in the right soil.

The Japanese snowbell gets its name from its dainty white flowers with upturned tips.

The golden-yellow foliage of 'Standishii' brightens a shady spot in the yard all year round.

YEW 'STANDISHII' *TAXUS BACCATA* 'STANDISHII'

HEIGHT & SPREAD up to 6 × 3¼ft (1.8 × 1m)
SOIL Well-drained
HARDINESS Zones 6–8

SUN ☀ ☀ ☀
PRUNING TIME Pruning is not needed
SHAPE 🌲 🌳

'Standishii' is a slow-growing yew tree that is ideal for a dry, shady part of the garden. It is also a good choice for an urban space, because it tolerates air pollution very well. It has an erect habit, holding its branches almost vertically, with no central leader, so that the top of the tree has several points rather like a crown. Older trees become more broadly columnar, but it can take 50 years for them to reach their ultimate height. The evergreen foliage is leathery and narrow with a distinct central midrib, and golden-yellow all year round. The flowers are insignificant, but red berries (technically "arils") are sometimes borne on older plants in the fall. These are fleshy, with a matte skin. Although popular with birds, the berries are toxic for people and pets, as is the foliage, so wear gloves when handling the tree.

TREE CARE Water newly planted trees regularly while their roots establish, but once mature, 'Standishii' will tolerate long periods of drought. It is very hardy and will be happy in a sheltered or exposed position of any aspect. It does not need any pruning but can be lightly clipped in summer to trim it into a neater shape. Should snow settle on the branches in winter, shake it off to avoid the weight irreparably bending the tree out of shape or even breaking branches.

'Elsrijk' is an especially neat variety of field maple with a compact crown that makes it suitable for small spaces.

FIELD MAPLE 'ELSRIJK' *ACER CAMPESTRE* 'ELSRIJK'

HEIGHT & SPREAD 33 × 20ft (10 × 6m)
SOIL Moist but well-drained
HARDINESS Zones 5–8

SUN ☼ ☽
PRUNING TIME Winter
SHAPE 🌲

'Elsrijk' is a variety of field maple that was bred to be a successful street tree in urban locations, where dry, cold winds can be just as much of a problem as on exposed hillsides. It has a slender habit, with a narrow crown, and can therefore fit into small spaces. It also copes well with compacted soil, urban air pollution, coastal conditions, and periods of flooding. The dense crown of deciduous foliage casts a good amount of shade; the leaves are three-lobed, mid-green in spring, darkening through summer and then turning a rich, buttery yellow in autumn. Inconspicuous flowers in spring, especially useful for pollinators, are followed by paired seeds with "helicopter" wings ("samaras") in autumn. The tree supports a wide range of wildlife: insects feed on its leaves and flowers, and subsequently, other insects and birds feed on them, while other species of birds and small mammals enjoy the seeds.

TREE CARE This robust tree will grow well in all soil types and situations; plant it in full sun or partial shade. Water newly planted trees regularly while they establish their roots, especially during dry or windy spells. Take out any damaged, dead, and diseased branches that need removing in early winter.

ITALIAN ALDER *ALNUS CORDATA*

HEIGHT & SPREAD 39 × 10ft (12 × 3m)
SOIL Moist/moist but well-drained
HARDINESS Zones 5–9

SUN ☼
PRUNING TIME Winter
SHAPE 🌲

The Italian alder is an upright, narrowly conical tree, its branches held almost perpendicular to the trunk, giving it a strong and architectural winter form. It is ideal as a windbreak, because it grows vigorously even in exposed areas where it is subject to strong winds. The leaves are dark green and glossy, an elongated heart-shape with lighter-colored veins and slightly toothed edges; there is no significant fall color. In late winter and early spring the tree produces catkins that hang in small bunches from the bare branches. The male catkins are around 4in (10cm) long, bright yellow fading to brown, while the females are shorter, rounder, and green. Once pollinated, the latter turn brown and harden into conelike seed pods; the seeds are popular with many birds.

TREE CARE Italian alders are easy-going and grow in a wide range of sites but prefer full sun and a moist soil. They tolerate poor and compacted soils, dry conditions, alkaline or chalky soils (see pp.26–27), and urban air pollution. Water young trees regularly while their roots establish. In early to midwinter, while the tree is dormant, remove any damaged, dead, or diseased branches and, if necessary, take out any other branches that are spoiling the overall shape of the crown at the same time.

Both male and female catkins are produced on Italian alder trees, the females providing seeds for birds.

Hawthorn flowers are also known as May flowers or May blossoms, named after the month in which they appear.

COMMON HAWTHORN *CRATAEGUS MONOGYNA*

HEIGHT & SPREAD up to 20 × 20ft (6 × 6m)
SOIL Well-drained/moist but well-drained
HARDINESS Zones 5–7

SUN ☼ ☼
PRUNING TIME Winter
SHAPE 🌳

The hawthorn is a slow-growing, thorny tree that is popular with wildlife for its blossom and fruits, known as haws. The trunk and branches become gnarled with age and in exposed locations will grow away from the prevailing wind, giving them a characterful, windswept appearance that is more pronounced in exposed situations. The rounded crown of deciduous foliage is made up of small, three-lobed leaves that emerge bright green in spring before the flowers, maturing to a darker green in summer. The fall foliage is undistinguished. The branches are smothered with sprays of creamy-white blossoms in spring, followed by the plentiful haws in late summer and fall. Where they have not been eaten by birds and small mammals or picked to make into haw ketchup or hedgerow jelly, the haws will persist on the branches into winter.

TREE CARE Planted in any aspect as a specimen or boundary tree, hawthorns will handle exposure to winds and coastal conditions very well. They also tolerate urban air pollution and sites in partial shade. Water young trees while they establish their roots; mature trees need very little maintenance. If necessary, damaged or dead branches can be pruned out in winter.

AUTUMN OLIVE *ELAEAGNUS UMBELLATA*

HEIGHT & SPREAD 16 × 16ft (5 × 5m)
SOIL Well-drained/moist but well-drained
HARDINESS Zones 4–9

SUN ☼
PRUNING TIME Winter
SHAPE 🌳

Also known as the autumn oleaster, the autumn olive is a bushy, deciduous small tree or large shrub that is particularly suited to windy and coastal sites in warm areas. Its narrowly ovate, wavy-edged leaves unfurl with a silvery sheen that fades to mid-green on the upper side of the leaf but is retained on the underside. Creamy-yellow tubular flowers with four-pointed petals and a strong, spicy fragrance open in spring, borne in clusters that hang from the underside of the branches. A profusion of small, berrylike fruits follows them; these are gray-green to begin with, ripening to red, and are popular with birds and other wildlife. They are also edible for people and can be eaten raw (only when fully ripe, as they are mouth-puckeringly astringent when underripe) or made into preserves.

TREE CARE The autumn olive will thrive in all soils except very chalky conditions (see pp.26–27) and will do best in full sun. Water young trees regularly after planting until the roots are established. They should need little or no pruning, but dead, damaged, and diseased branches can be removed in late winter if necessary. Wear protective clothing, including a face mask, when working on the tree, as the leaves can have a powdery coating that creates an unpleasant cloud of dust when disturbed.

The creamy-yellow tubular flowers of the autumn olive are rich in nectar for pollinators in spring.

HOLM OAK *QUERCUS ILEX*

HEIGHT & SPREAD Up to 82 × 66ft (25 × 20m)
SOIL Well-drained/moist but well-drained
HARDINESS Zones 7–10

SUN ☀️
PRUNING TIME Summer
SHAPE 🌳

The holm oak is a slow-growing evergreen tree with a large, rounded crown. Although it can eventually reach gargantuan proportions, it is easily clipped to a required shape and size and can even be grown as a hedge. The leaves are ovate with a pointed tip and distinct central midrib, glossy dark green on the upper side and gray-green and hairy on the underside. The young foliage is silvery-gray. Yellow catkins in spring are followed by rounded, dark brown acorns in the fall. Both the foliage and acorns are toxic for pets if ingested. In recent years trees have been affected by some invasive pests, so buy a certified healthy tree from a reputable nursery.

TREE CARE The holm oak grows on all soils and does well with coastal and windy conditions but requires mild temperatures and will not thrive in colder, inland areas that experience harsh winters. The oldest leaves will yellow and fall in summer, but this is a natural annual process. Water young trees while they are establishing; mature trees should not need watering if grown in the right soil. No pruning is necessary except formative shaping of the branches and removal of damaged or dead branches on mature trees. Prune in mid- to late summer to avoid subsequent new growth being damaged by cold weather.

The glossy coating on holm oak leaves protects them from salty coastal spray and winds.

COMMON WHITEBEAM *SORBUS ARIA*

HEIGHT & SPREAD 26 × 13ft (8 × 4m)
SOIL Well-drained/moist but well-drained
HARDINESS Zones 4–8

SUN ☀️☀️
PRUNING TIME Winter
SHAPE 🌳

The common whitebeam is an upright, deciduous tree with a neat, rounded crown. Although it doesn't need any maintenance pruning, it can be pruned to a more compact shape, or even trained, such as to form an archway when planted as a pair on either side of a path. The leaves are a broad oval shape, deeply ridged with veins and slightly serrated along their edges; they are gray-green on the top, white beneath, and covered with a downy felt that helps them handle dry soils and exposed, polluted, and windy conditions. In the fall they turn shades of russet and red. They are a caterpillar food plant for many moth species. White flowers useful for pollinators appear in spring, followed in early autumn by red berries (also known as chess apples) that are popular with birds.

TREE CARE This is a low-maintenance tree that tolerates an exposed position well. It grows on most soils, including chalk, but prefers moist, fertile conditions. Water young trees regularly, especially during dry spells, but mature trees should need little maintenance. If there are any damaged, diseased, or dead branches, these can be removed in winter while the tree is dormant. Formative pruning on young trees will help shape a balanced framework.

The neat crowns of whitebeam trees make them ideal for planting along a boundary next to a road.

SWEDISH WHITEBEAM *SORBUS INTERMEDIA*

HEIGHT & SPREAD up to 39 x 39ft (12 x 12m)
SOIL Well-drained/moist but well-drained
HARDINESS Zones 4–8
SUN ☼ ☼
PRUNING TIME Winter
SHAPE 🌳

The Swedish whitebeam is a very tolerant and tough tree that forms a dense, rounded crown of deciduous foliage on a slender trunk. The leaves are consistently the same color from spring to fall: a rich, deep green on the top with a lighter, softly hairy underside that gives the tree an overall silvery appearance. They are a wide oval shape with rounded lobes around their edges. In spring, the tree bears profuse, flat-topped clusters of small single white flowers. These are followed by red berries that are popular with wildlife and don't last long on the tree where there are large populations of birds. 'Brouwers' is a good medium-sized variety that forms a more uniformly oval crown than the species.

TREE CARE The Swedish whitebeam is happy in most garden soils, and while it will grow best in a moist but well-drained, moderately fertile soil, it will tolerate drier conditions. It will grow in full sun or partial shade and tolerates exposure to wind, cold, urban air pollution, and coastal spray. Water young trees regularly while the roots establish. Prune during winter while the tree is dormant, but only to remove damaged, dead, or diseased branches or to rebalance the crown after wind damage.

The Swedish whitebeam is a compact and neat medium or large tree with a crown of silvery leaves.

The four-stamen tamarisk flowers are borne in large, showy, pink plumes that rustle gently in the breeze.

FOUR-STAMEN TAMARISK *TAMARIX TETANDRA*

HEIGHT & SPREAD Up to 13 x 13ft (4 x 4m)
SOIL Well-drained/moist but well-drained
HARDINESS Zones 5–9
SUN ☼
PRUNING TIME Winter
SHAPE 🌳

The four-stamen tamarisk is a small, spreading tree, either multi-stemmed or growing from a short trunk. It is an architectural addition to a garden and suits many different garden styles. The branches are upright but lax, arching gracefully outward at the ends; they are nearly black, and the leaves that grow on the fingerlike branchlets are tiny green scales. This adaptation reduces water loss in dry and windy conditions, making it an excellent choice for an exposed position—its alternative name of salt cedar indicates its propensity to grow near the sea. In late spring the tree is covered in long, cascading plumes of pale pink flowers, individually small but en masse creating a dramatic effect. They are followed by small fruits containing the seeds.

TREE CARE The four-stamen tamarisk dislikes shallow, chalky soil and prefers well-drained, sandy soil, in full sun or dappled shade and the milder temperatures of coastal locations. It will not do well in areas with very cold and wet winters; shelter it from drying winds in colder inland climates. Water newly planted trees while they are establishing, but mature trees will not need any irrigation. Tamarisk do not require any pruning, but dead or broken branches can be taken out in late winter.

Trees that lend themselves to regular pruning, such as bay (*Laurus nobilis*), can be cut annually to maintain their small size.

TREES FOR SMALL SPACES

Naturally compact species as well as trees that have been bred to maintain their small size are ideal for yards where space is at a premium. Some will even thrive in a large pot if watered and fed regularly, while fruit trees are available on a range of dwarfing rootstocks that limit their proportions, allowing you to grow your own apples and pears in a courtyard or even up on a roof. So, although your space may be limited, there are plenty of trees that will suit it.

BOX ELDER 'FLAMINGO' *ACER NEGUNDO* 'FLAMINGO'

HEIGHT & SPREAD 13 × 10ft (4 × 3m)
SOIL Moist but well-drained
HARDINESS Zones 2–9

SUN ☼ ☼
PRUNING TIME Winter
SHAPE ▲

This variety gets its name from the pink variegation on the young leaves as they emerge in spring. Combined with the vivid red leaf stems, they make it a striking addition to the garden. As the leaves mature in summer, the pink fades to a creamy white, and in the fall the foliage is golden yellow. Ornamental gray-white bark on the trunk and stems adds winter interest; the green-yellow flowers in spring are insignificant, although beneficial to pollinating insects.

Plant next to darker-leaved trees and shrubs or a dark-colored wall or fence to bring out the hues to their full extent. 'Flamingo' is less vigorous than the species but will still grow relatively quickly; its slender habit and narrow canopy are well-suited to a small or medium-sized yard.

TREE CARE This tree is hardier than many ornamental acers and will grow well in most soils and situations, provided they are not too exposed; a very sunny or windy position can result in the leaves getting scorched. Water regularly as the tree is establishing. The only pruning needed is to remove any dead, diseased, or damaged shoots in winter, though pruning back to a framework of short stems each winter will encourage larger leaves. Prune any fully green ("reverted") shoots back to the main stem in summer.

The pink and white foliage of 'Flamingo' lends itself to both modern and traditional planting schemes.

SNOWY MESPILUS *AMELANCHIER LAMARCKII*

HEIGHT & SPREAD 26 × 13ft (8 × 4m)
SOIL Moist but well-drained
HARDINESS Zones 4–8

SUN ☼ ☼
PRUNING TIME Winter
SHAPE ▲

Snowy mespilus gains its name from its white blossoms, which are so profuse the trees look as if they are covered in snow.

Also known as Juneberry or serviceberry, this deciduous tree has a long season of ornamental interest, making it a good choice for a small yard. In spring, the branches erupt into bloom, each flower a delicate star shape, but they are so profusely borne that the overall effect is a frothy explosion, set off by the bronze young leaves. The foliage matures to green and then turns a vibrant orange-red in the fall. This tree grows quickly, with an upright, many-branched habit. Several in a row form an excellent screen or high hedge. Other *Amelanchier* species are very similar; for a more upright, narrow tree, try *A. alnifolia* 'Obelisk'.

Amelanchier species are excellent choices for a wildlife-friendly yard. The blossom provides a good source of early nectar and pollen for bees and other insects, while the berries that follow in summer are extremely popular with birds.

TREE CARE The snowy mespilus prefers neutral to acidic soils and won't grow well in alkaline (limy) ones but is not fussy about other garden conditions. It tolerates partial shade, but plant it in a sunnier position for the best fall color. It requires very little pruning; just cut wayward stems in late winter or early spring.

CHINESE REDBUD 'AVONDALE' *CERCIS CHINENSIS 'AVONDALE'*

HEIGHT & SPREAD 8 x 5ft (2.5 x 1.5m)
SOIL Moist but well-drained
HARDINESS Zones 6–9

SUN ☼ ☼
PRUNING TIME Winter
SHAPE 🌳

'Avondale' is a particularly compact variety of redbud well-suited to small spaces and courtyards; it can even be grown in a large pot. It naturally forms a rounded, bushy shape, but its multi-stemmed habit also makes it suitable for training against a wall. In spring it puts on a generous display of intense pink flowers, borne on the bare branches, that will effectively dispel the last of any gray winter gloom. The large, heart-shaped leaves have a reddish-purple tint as they unfurl, making a good foil for other garden plants, and turn yellow in the fall. A reliable ornamental small tree, 'Avondale' is also a good choice for an urban wildlife garden: *Cercis* are in the pea family, plants known for their particularly good-quality nectar and pollen.

TREE CARE *Cercis* will flower best in a sunny position but will also tolerate some shade. They are not fussy about soil type and will grow well in most situations. If planting in a pot, use a large container, 20in (50cm) in diameter, filled with a peat-free, soil-based potting mix. Water newly planted trees in the ground regularly until their roots establish; those in pots will need regular watering and a liquid fertilizer in spring and summer. Prune in winter to remove dead, diseased, or damaged branches.

Training a Chinese redbud against a sunny wall shows off the vivid flowers to their best advantage.

CORNELIAN CHERRY *CORNUS MAS*

HEIGHT & SPREAD 8 x 8ft (2.5 x 2.5m)
SOIL Moist but well-drained
HARDINESS Zones 5–8

SUN ☼ ☼
PRUNING TIME Winter
SHAPE 🌳

The cornelian cherry's flowers may be small, but their profusion brings cheer to the garden in late winter.

The cornelian cherry does indeed have cherrylike fruits: glossy and red, they appear in late summer and fall against a background of purple-green foliage. Clusters of tiny yellow flowers emerge in late winter on bare branches and persist for some time, providing a valuable early source of food for bumblebees. The fruits, borne in abundance, are popular with birds; if you'd also like to eat them (adding a lot of sugar to make them palatable), try the cultivars 'Golden Glory' or 'Kasanlaker', which are both slightly larger than the species, reaching 10ft (3m) in height and spread. This tree has a spreading, open habit; to better see the multi-stemmed framework in summer, you could prune off the lower branches to expose more of it (known as "crown-lifting").

TREE CARE Cornelian cherries are reliable, low-maintenance trees that are relatively slow-growing. They prefer a rich, deep soil but tolerate most soils and aspects. Those placed in full sun will flower and fruit best. Water young trees regularly, especially during dry spells, until their roots are established. Prune out dead, damaged, or diseased branches in winter while the tree is dormant. You can also take out or shorten branches to produce a balanced framework or to reduce the tree's size if required.

The yellow catkins hang like tassels from the bare branches of the corkscrew hazel in spring.

CORKSCREW HAZEL *CORYLUS AVELLANA* 'CONTORTA'

HEIGHT & SPREAD 13 x 13ft (4 x 4m)
SOIL Moist but well-drained
HARDINESS Zones 4–8

SUN ☼ ☼
PRUNING TIME Winter
SHAPE 🌳

The twisted stems of the corkscrew hazel are very decorative and can be used in cut-flower arrangements and festive decorations, both in winter when the stems are bare and in spring when they are adorned with yellow catkins. The leaves are large and rounded, deep green in summer, turning yellow in autumn; also available is the variety 'Red Majestic', with red leaves and catkins. The tree's contorted stems make it suited to a wide range of garden styles; plant where you can enjoy its structure in winter. As a hazel tree, it may bear nuts in late summer and early fall, which birds and squirrels will enjoy; it is also used by butterflies as a larval food plant.

TREE CARE Corkscrew hazel trees are tolerant of a wide range of soils and situations and will grow well in both dappled shade and full sun. They form a small, shrublike, multi-stemmed tree that is easy to shape as you wish by taking out branches to form either a shorter, wider plant or a taller, narrower one. After you have had the benefit of the attractive dangling catkins in spring, cut any unwanted, dead, or damaged branches back to the main stem or to the ground and shorten others. Water young trees while they are still establishing; once they are mature, these trees need little other maintenance.

MAGNOLIA 'LEONARD MESSEL' *MAGNOLIA × LOEBNERI* 'LEONARD MESSEL'

HEIGHT & SPREAD 20 x 20ft (6 x 6m)
SOIL Moist but well-drained
HARDINESS Zones 5–9

SUN ☼ ☼
PRUNING TIME Winter
SHAPE 🌳

The scented flowers of this magnolia are around 4in (10cm) across and are borne in profusion on the bare branches in mid-spring, making it a spectacular and elegant tree for any garden. The buds are a blush pink on the outside; once open, the petals are pale pink, almost white, and form a star shape. The flowers on 'Leonard Messel' are less susceptible than other magnolias to damage by frost. The leaves that follow stay green into the fall and are long and pointed. Although 'Leonard Messel' can reach 20ft (6m) or more in height and spread, it is a slow-growing tree and will take up to 50 years to reach that size.

TREE CARE While magnolias are hardy, they need a position protected from harsh winds and the worst of the winter cold. As a species they prefer neutral or acidic soil (see p.26), but 'Leonard Messel' will tolerate more alkaline or chalky conditions. Prune between midsummer and early fall if required, removing only dead, diseased, or damaged wood. To reduce the size or thin the branches on older trees, carry out the changes over a few years rather than all at once to avoid stressing the tree. Water young trees regularly, especially in dry spells, while the roots are establishing. They may not reach their full flowering potential until they are mature.

The scented flowers of 'Leonard Messel' are more easily appreciated within the confines of a small yard.

Even young crab apple trees produce a lot of blossoms in spring, turning the tree's crown white and pink.

CRAB APPLE 'EVERESTE' *MALUS* 'EVERESTE'

HEIGHT & SPREAD 13 × 13ft (4 × 4m)
SOIL Moist but well-drained
HARDINESS Zones 3–8

SUN ☼ ☼
PRUNING TIME Winter
SHAPE 🌲

Crab apples are hard-working but charming trees for a small space. Their large white spring flowers open from pinkish-red buds and are popular with bees and other insects. These trees are also good pollinator partners for eating apples; the blossom on 'Evereste' is particularly abundant. In the fall, the miniature apples, which are held on the branches in pendulous bunches, ripen to a reddish-yellow. They are tart but edible, often used to make crab apple jelly. Alternatively, they can be left on the tree, where they will stay well into winter, providing food for wildlife, in particular blackbirds. The neat, conical habit of this compact tree makes it well suited to small spaces. Planted in a front yard, it will tolerate air pollution and provide screening as well.

TREE CARE Crab apples grow well in most soils. They are hardy enough to withstand any aspect and some exposure to winds, although avoid planting in a frost pocket, as freezing temperatures will damage the blossom. Water young trees regularly while the roots are establishing. After pruning to create a balanced framework (see p.129), only minimal pruning is needed each winter while the tree is dormant. Just remove any broken, diseased, or dead branches and any that are crossing or badly placed.

FUJI CHERRY *PRUNUS INCISA*

HEIGHT & SPREAD 13–26 × 6½–10ft (4–8 × 2–3m)
SOIL Moist but well-drained
HARDINESS Zones 6–8

SUN ☼
PRUNING TIME Summer
SHAPE 🌳 🌳 🌴

This species of ornamental cherry is relatively compact and a good choice for smaller spaces. The blossom of a tree planted in a front yard can cheer the whole street, but they are well suited to a range of locations. *P. incisa* f. *yamadei* is an umbrella-shaped tree with white flowers; *P. incisa* 'Pendula' is similarly weeping in habit, also with white flowers; 'Praecox' has white flowers in late winter and is broadly spreading; 'Kojo-no-mai' is a dwarf, more rounded, and shrublike plant with pale pink flowers. All will put on a beautiful display of blossoms in the spring and light up the garden later with red-orange autumn foliage. These varieties are all single-flowered, too, and are recommended over double-flowered varieties because pollinators can access the nectar and pollen in them more easily.

TREE CARE Plant Fuji cherries in full sun for the best flowers and fall color. They will grow in most soils but prefer a relatively sheltered position. Water newly planted trees regularly, especially in dry spells, for at least two years while their roots establish. Prune in summer to prevent silver leaf disease, which is more prevalent in the fall and winter. Remove any dead, diseased, damaged, or misplaced branches to maintain a balanced framework.

The Fuji cherry is more compact than other spring-flowering cherry trees, but just as floriferous.

ASCENDING WEEPING CHERRY 'ROSEA' *PRUNUS PENDULA F. ASCENDENS 'ROSEA'*

HEIGHT & SPREAD 10 × 6½ft (3 × 2m)
SOIL Moist but well-drained
HARDINESS Zones 6–8

SUN ☼
PRUNING TIME Summer
SHAPE ▮

This ornamental cherry tree, also known as *P. subhirtella* 'Rosea', has a slender, upright, vase-shaped form that suits narrow spaces. Plant singly or put several in a row alongside a fence or wall, or in a front yard, to provide screening. Ornamental cherries are best known for their masses of blossoms in early spring, before the leaves emerge. 'Rosea' has rose- or shell-pink flowers with a deep pink center that open from red buds and fade to a pale pink, almost white, as they age. They are single flowers, giving easy access to the nectar for insects, and are held in clusters, flowering on wood that is at least one year old. In autumn this beautiful tree lights up the garden again, this time with fiery foliage, when the deep green leaves turn a brilliant reddish-orange.

TREE CARE Ornamental cherries flower best and produce the brightest autumn color when planted in a sunny, relatively sheltered position. They will grow well in most soils. Water newly planted trees regularly for at least two years after planting while their roots establish, especially during dry spells. Prune if necessary in summer, which helps prevent silver leaf disease. Remove dead, diseased, or damaged branches and take out any that are misplaced to keep a balanced framework.

The upright branches of 'Rosea' burst into bloom on bare stems and offer a feast for pollinating insects.

BLACK LOCUST 'LACE LADY' *ROBINIA PSEUDOACACIA 'LACE LADY'*

HEIGHT & SPREAD 10 × 6½ft (3 × 2m)
SOIL Well-drained/moist but well-drained
HARDINESS Zones 4–9

SUN ☼ ☼
PRUNING TIME Late summer/early autumn
SHAPE 🌳

The curling leaves and pendulous branches of 'Lacy Lady' add textural interest to the garden.

While other black locusts can form large, fast-growing trees, this is a slow-growing dwarf form that suits a smaller garden much better. At 10 years old, a tree may reach only 5 × 4ft (1.5 × 1.2m) in height and spread. It is also relatively tolerant of dry conditions, which makes it a good choice for a gravel garden, although its architectural form would add interest to any garden style. 'Lace Lady' is also known as 'Twisty Baby', which refers to the form of the leaves and stems; the latter are contorted, while the leaves have a delicate curl. Each leaf is made up of many pairs of small leaflets, emerging acid green in spring, deepening to a mid-green for summer, then turning golden-yellow in the fall. The twisted bare branches add winter interest.

TREE CARE Water young trees regularly while their roots establish, especially during dry spells. Pruning is not necessary, but dead, diseased, and broken stems can be removed if required. You may also wish to take out any misplaced branches that are affecting the look and framework of the tree. Prune in late summer or early autumn when there will be minimal sap bleeding, wearing gloves to protect your hands from thorns. Remove any suckers (young shoots from the base) at the same time.

HOP TREE *PTELEA TRIFOLIATA*

HEIGHT & SPREAD 26 × 13ft (8 × 4m)
SOIL Well-drained
HARDINESS Zones 4–9

SUN ☼ ☼
PRUNING TIME Winter
SHAPE 🌳

All parts of the hop tree—flowers, leaves, and bark—are wonderfully aromatic. It forms a rounded, spreading, shrublike tree that could be planted near a path or doorway to best appreciate the fragrance. The leaves are large and dark green, formed of three parts held on a long stalk. Sprays of tiny yellow-white flowers that are attractive to butterflies appear in summer, followed by clusters of pale green, winged seeds; each one is surrounded by a thin disc about 1in (2.5cm) across that helps it blow away in the wind, dispersing the seeds effectively. The seeds are held on the tree into winter, turning a chocolate-brown color before being released.

They were once used as a substitute for real hops (*Humulus lupulus*) in brewing. The variety 'Aurea' has leaves that emerge bright yellow in spring, fading to a yellow-green in summer.

TREE CARE As they are untroubled by pests and diseases, hop trees are low-maintenance. Plant in full sun or dappled shade and water consistently for the first two or three years while the roots establish. The tree requires little to no pruning: check in winter for any diseased, dead, or broken branches and remove these. More branches could be taken out to create a better shape if desired.

The lime-green seed casings turn a chocolate brown in winter and are held on the branches long after the leaves fall.

Coyote willow makes an attractive and architectural tree for planting among perennials.

COYOTE WILLOW *SALIX EXIGUA*

HEIGHT & SPREAD 13 × 13ft (4 × 4m)
SOIL Moist but well-drained
HARDINESS Zones 4–6

SUN ☼ ☼
PRUNING TIME Winter
SHAPE 🌳

This willow has attractive 4in (10cm) long leaves, emerging silver in spring and fading to a gray-green color in summer, which make an excellent foil for other plants and flowers. Each leaf is covered in a down of soft, fine hairs. The catkins, which are produced in spring along with the young leaves, are a yellowish-gray color and a good source of early pollen for both honeybees and bumblebees. The stems are slender and upright, all growing from the base to form a thicket that is ideal for screening an ugly feature. It's also possible to prune the plant so that all the stems emerge from a single trunk (a "leg").

TREE CARE Coyote willow is fast-growing but is easily pruned back hard when necessary to keep it to size. In late winter, take out any dead, damaged, or diseased shoots back to the base or the top of the leg. Also remove any suckers (new shoots that pop up in the ground around the plant) by digging or cutting them out to prevent the tree from spreading sideways. Trees that have been hard pruned will shoot anew, putting on around 3¼ft (1m) or more of fresh growth that year. Water young trees regularly as they establish their roots. Support trees grown on a leg with a short stake for a few years until the leg thickens.

Lifting the crown of the tree shows off its twisted trunks and allows for planting perennials beneath.

STRAWBERRY TREE *ARBUTUS UNEDO*

HEIGHT & SPREAD 13 × 10ft (4 × 3m)
SOIL Well-drained
HARDINESS Zones 7–10

SUN ☼
PRUNING TIME Winter
SHAPE 🌳

The strawberry tree is a Mediterranean plant and thus an ideal choice for a courtyard or other sheltered garden where it will be protected from cold winds. Its dense, rounded crown of leathery, mid-green leaves contrast well with the reddish-brown bark, which peels attractively after a few years. As the tree ages, it becomes gnarled and architectural in shape. Unusually, it can be in fruit and flower at the same time. The round, strawberry-like fruits develop from the previous year's blooms, ripening from pale green to scarlet in the fall; they are edible but not tasty and are best left for birds. The diminutive, nodding white flowers are bell-shaped. A smaller variety of the strawberry tree, 'Compacta', reaches just 6½ft (2m) in height and spread.

TREE CARE Plant in a site sheltered from cold winds and a soil that is not prone to waterlogging; a mature tree can survive temperatures down to 5°F (−15°C), but young trees may not survive a very cold winter. Water regularly for their first two years. After that, they need little attention and are relatively free of pests and diseases. Choose a single or multi-stemmed tree; neither will require much pruning apart from removing dead, diseased, and crossing stems after the frosts in spring.

LAWSON'S CYPRESS 'MINIMA AUREA' *CHAMAECYPARIS LAWSONIANA* 'MINIMA AUREA'

HEIGHT & SPREAD 3¼ × 3¼ft (1 × 1m)
SOIL Moist but well-drained
HARDINESS Zones 5–7

SUN ☼
PRUNING TIME Pruning is not needed
SHAPE 🌲

This conifer forms a slightly squat, dwarf cone of soft, textural foliage. It has an architectural shape that lends itself both to punctuating more billowing plants in borders and for using in formal schemes. Alternatively, plant as a specimen tree or use two or more symmetrically around an entrance or path. Very slow-growing, taking up to 50 years to reach its full height of 3¼ft (1m), 'Minima Aurea' can be used to add evergreen interest and structure to small gardens. The dense foliage is golden-green, held in upright, flattened sprays, the color brighter and more pronounced in younger trees. In winter, the colder temperatures cause the foliage to take on a richer hue.

TREE CARE Plant in full sun for the best golden color; trees planted in shadier spots will have darker green foliage. They tolerate a range of soils but prefer conditions that are slightly acidic (see p.26). Water newly planted trees regularly for at least the first two years while their roots establish. They are very low-maintenance, requiring no pruning at all. However, if you want to shape the foliage, you can trim it in both spring and summer with hedging shears. Wear gloves and long sleeves when working with or near the tree, as the foliage may cause skin irritation. Aphids can cause damage to the foliage, causing it to die back.

The foliage of 'Minima Aurea' is held in loose, bushy clumps, which add texture and form to the garden.

Each year 'Cornubia' produces thousands of scarlet berries, which are loved by birds.

COTONEASTER 'CORNUBIA' *COTONEASTER* 'CORNUBIA'

HEIGHT & SPREAD 20 × 13ft (6 × 4m)
SOIL Well-drained
HARDINESS Zones 5–8

SUN ☀
PRUNING TIME Spring
SHAPE 🌳

Most cotoneaster species are shrubs, as indeed 'Cornubia' can be, but trained into a form with a single trunk, it can also make an attractive small tree. The long, arching branches form an umbrella-like crown and become more pendulous in the fall under the weight of the berries; the leaves are a deep green, taking on a bronze tint in autumn. In early to midsummer the tree is covered in spectacular masses of white flowers, each a large, flat spray of small individual blooms that are strongly scented and extremely popular with bees, butterflies, and other insects. The bundles of vivid scarlet berries are held on the branches from the fall into winter and are a useful food source for birds (but toxic for humans). In colder areas, the tree may be semi-evergreen, losing some of its leaves over winter.

TREE CARE Plant in a sheltered spot in full sun, especially in northern areas. 'Cornubia' tolerates most well-drained soils, but not those that become waterlogged. It will need regular watering when young until its roots establish. Prune to form a plant with a single trunk and a balanced crown of branches, but thereafter keep pruning to a minimum, removing only dead, damaged, or diseased stems each year in summer after flowering.

HOLLY *ILEX AQUIFOLIUM*

HEIGHT & SPREAD up to 20 × 10ft (6 × 3m)
SOIL Moist but well-drained
HARDINESS Zones 5–9

SUN ☀ ◑
PRUNING TIME Summer
SHAPE 🌲 🌲

Holly is relatively slow-growing and easily shaped, making it a good choice for a small garden. Its leaves are dark green, glossy, and generally prickly. Unremarkable small white flowers in summer are followed by bright red berries in late fall and winter, but only on pollinated female and self-fertile varieties—male trees will not produce them. The berries are toxic to humans but popular with birds. A number of compact varieties have been introduced: 'Alaska' is narrowly conical, reaching 10ft (3m); 'Aurea Marginata' is compact and bushy, around 13ft (4m) tall, with a yellow variegation to the leaf edges; 'Green Pillar' forms a narrowly conical shape and reaches 10ft (3m) tall; 'Siberia' is conical, with an ultimate height of 16ft (5m); 'Silver Queen' is similar to 'Aurea Marginata' but with a white variegation.

TREE CARE Hollies fruit better in the sunshine but also grow well in dappled or partial shade. They tolerate all soils, provided they are not waterlogged. Shape the crown by trimming with hedging shears or removing branches in late summer. Remove lower branches and any shoots from the base to form a clear trunk. Alternatively, leave the natural shape, pruning only to remove damaged, dead, or diseased branches, also in late summer.

'Silver Queen' has creamy-white edges to its leaves, which can brighten a dark corner of the garden.

COMMON JUNIPER 'GOLD CONE' *JUNIPERUS COMMUNIS* 'GOLD CONE'

HEIGHT & SPREAD 6½ × 3¼ft (2 × 1m)
SOIL Moist but well-drained
HARDINESS Zones 2–6

SUN ☀ ☀
PRUNING TIME Spring/summer
SHAPE 🌲

'Gold Cone' is an upright and compact conifer that is suited to a wide range of garden styles, adding evergreen structure to a mixed border or more formal planting schemes. As it will only reach its diminutive full height of 6½ft (2m) after around 10 years, it can be relied upon not to outgrow a small garden, and it requires very little maintenance. The branches are held vertically and relatively tightly, giving it an overall upright, columnar shape. The foliage is a green-gold color, with new growth in a brighter yellow, and overall becomes richer and brighter in color during the winter. It is also pleasantly scented.

TREE CARE Plant 'Gold Cone' in any soil and full sun or dappled shade; the color will be brighter in sunnier spots. In winter, protect it from strong winds, which can open up the branch structure and distort the overall form. Shake heavy snow off the branches so that they don't bend over or break. The tree requires no pruning except to remove any dead branches but can be given a light trim in spring and summer to give it a tighter shape or to form a spiraled cone. Conifers occasionally produce a second leader (the upmost, central shoot), which needs to be quickly removed so that the overall form does not become too wide at the top.

The bright foliage and evergreen structure of 'Gold Cone' can be used as a focal point amid lower-growing plants.

This bay tree has been trained and clipped as a standard to give evergreen structure to an herb garden.

BAY TREE *LAURUS NOBILIS*

HEIGHT & SPREAD up to 39 × 33ft (12 × 10m)
SOIL Well-drained/moist but well-drained
HARDINESS Zones 7–10

SUN ☀ ☀
PRUNING TIME Summer
SHAPE 🌳 🌱 🌲 🌲

Bay trees are very versatile plants—they can be grown as small cones no higher than your hip or allowed to form trees of any shape or size. Clipped into dense shapes, they suit a formal style perfectly but are at home in any space. Their aromatic, dark green leaves are a useful culinary herb, so try growing a tree in a large pot by your kitchen door. The small spring flowers are yellow-white and slightly fragrant, while the smooth bark is an attractive gray color.

TREE CARE Plant bay trees in well-drained soil and a sunny, sheltered spot where they will be protected from frosts and cold winds, which can cause them to lose leaves over winter. They will also tolerate partial or dappled shade. Water young trees regularly as their roots establish. Most gardeners keep bay trees to their preferred size and shape by regular clipping and pruning: they are often sold as lollipop-shaped standards, a profile that is easily maintained with annual clipping, but they can be pruned into other shapes too. Prune in early summer, taking shoots back to just above a leaf. Remove frost-damaged tips with pruners rather than shears to avoid cutting through the leaves, as the remaining parts will wither and die unattractively.

MAGNOLIA 'KAY PARRIS' *MAGNOLIA GRANDIFLORA* 'KAY PARRIS'

HEIGHT & SPREAD 13 × 8ft (4 × 2.5m)
SOIL Well-drained/moist but well-drained
HARDINESS Zones 7–9

SUN ☼ ☼
PRUNING TIME Spring
SHAPE 🌲

The leathery leaves of this evergreen magnolia are a glossy deep green on the top and velvety rusty brown on the underside. They are held at an upward angle from the branch, so both sides can be admired at once. The creamy-white, bowl-shaped flowers appear through summer into the fall, each up to 10in (25cm) across. Highly scented with lemon and spice, they close at night and, after two or three days, develop into conelike seedpods. The tree is compact, with dense foliage, and is relatively robust in cold temperatures compared with other magnolias. It grows quickly, producing flowers even on young trees, and is long-lived.

TREE CARE 'Kay Parris' requires little maintenance. Water newly planted trees regularly in their first two years as their roots establish. While they tolerate dry and alkaline soils, they prefer a moist but well-drained and neutral to slightly acidic soil (see p.26). Trees in a sheltered, sunny position will flower best; they can also be trained on a warm wall. Prune in spring, as the tree starts into growth again. It is only necessary to remove dead, diseased, and broken branches, but you can also prune any that are crossing or look unbalanced within the framework of the crown. Shorten the side shoots of wall-trained trees to three or four buds from the main branch.

The large white flowers of 'Kay Parris' contrast beautifully with the rusty-brown and dark green leaves.

DWARF MOUNTAIN PINE *PINUS MUGO*

HEIGHT & SPREAD 8 × 13ft (2.5 × 4m)
SOIL Well-drained
HARDINESS Zones 3–7

SUN ☼
PRUNING TIME Pruning is not needed
SHAPE 🌳

Birds and small mammals will enjoy the seeds of the pinecones, if you don't collect them yourself for decorations.

This compact, sculptural pine is an ideal choice for a small garden. It has evolved to handle the dry, cold, rocky screes of mountainsides and will therefore thrive in a gravel garden or similarly well-drained or exposed situation. The dense, bushy branches of dark green needles are a good foil for other plants and provide year-round color and structure in the garden as well as offering shelter for birds. When the canopy is lifted, the architectural form of the stems beneath is revealed. New growth is upright and known as "candles." The dwarf mountain pine flowers in spring; the bumpy brown flowers are popular with moths and other nighttime pollinating insects, and the tree then produces dark brown cones that ripen in the fall.

TREE CARE These pines are extremely low-maintenance, and after some initial watering in the first two or three years while the roots establish, will happily grow with no further intervention. Their shallow root system means they grow well in a relatively thin layer of soil. They can be pruned in early spring if you need to keep them within a certain space or remove a broken branch, but they do not require any routine pruning. To lift the canopy, simply cut off the lower branches.

Japanese maples are ideal trees for containers and make a statement plant for a sheltered courtyard.

JAPANESE MAPLE *ACER PALMATUM*

HEIGHT & SPREAD 8 × 8ft (2.5 × 2.5m)
SOIL Moist but well-drained
HARDINESS Zones 5–9

SUN ☼ ☀
PRUNING TIME Winter
SHAPE 🌳

Popular for their ornamental foliage and small stature, Japanese maples are low-maintenance and slow-growing, making them ideal for containers. The leaves are prone to scorch in the sun, especially if finely dissected; those of 'Bloodgood', one of the best and most reliable, are large and therefore less susceptible. They are a deep purple-red, brightening to a vivid scarlet in the fall. In spring the tree produces small purple flowers, followed in autumn by red seeds. Other good varieties include 'Orange Dream', which has bright green bark and leaves that emerge yellow in spring, turn green for the summer, and then back to an orange-yellow in the fall. The foliage of 'Katsura' follows a similar seasonal pattern, but has narrower leaves.

TREE CARE Plant in a pot of at least 20in (50cm) in diameter, using soil-based, peat-free potting mix. Water regularly, ensuring the potting mix does not dry out. The leaves will brown and wither at the edges (scorch) if the tree is too dry at the roots or exposed to drying winds or too much sun. A sheltered spot with dappled shade is ideal. Repot every other year with fresh potting mix and apply a liquid fertilizer in summer. Prune in late winter, but only to remove damaged, dead, and diseased branches.

EASTERN REDBUD *CERCIS CANADENSIS*

HEIGHT & SPREAD 26 × 13ft (8 × 4m)
SOIL Moist but well-drained
HARDINESS Zones 5–9

SUN ☼ ☀
PRUNING TIME Winter
SHAPE 🌳

Eastern redbuds are very pretty trees for any small garden. They generally have multiple trunks, on which the branches are held almost horizontally in a flattened, spreading crown. In spring, the bare stems erupt with clusters of pink-purple flowers that are especially nutrient-rich for pollinators. The young foliage is bronze-tinted, maturing to green for the summer and then turning yellow in the fall. Green, bean-shaped seed pods appear in summer, then darken to brown, hanging from the branches into winter. Named cultivars have varying shades of foliage, but all have papery, heart-shaped leaves. Although eastern redbud trees can reach many feet in height and spread, they are very slow-growing and can be kept in a container for many years, where the restricted root space limits their growth further.

TREE CARE Plant your tree in a container 20in (50cm) in diameter, filled with a peat-free, soil-based potting mix. Repot every other year to refresh the potting mix. Water regularly to keep moist and apply a liquid fertilizer in spring and summer. Prune in winter to remove any dead, diseased, or damaged branches, also cutting out any misplaced stems if need be. Eastern redbuds flower best in a sunny position, but will also tolerate some shade.

The heart-shaped leaves of the Eastern redbud offer an evolving range of colors from spring to fall.

FLOWERING DOGWOOD *CORNUS FLORIDA*

HEIGHT & SPREAD 13 × 13ft (4 × 4m)
SOIL Moist but well-drained
HARDINESS Zones 5–9

SUN ☼ ☼
PRUNING TIME Winter
SHAPE 🌳

Flowering dogwoods can be grown in a pot for many years, as they are very slow in growth. This deciduous plant forms a small, spreading tree, its bare stems adding winter structure to the garden. The interesting, gray-patterned bark is more obvious at this time, but the main show is in late spring and early summer when the blooms appear. These consist of small green flowers surrounded by four large white bracts that resemble petals. Mature trees are often smothered in blooms every year. The foliage is a bright mid-green, turning red and purple in the fall. Cherrylike red fruits hang from long stalks all summer and into autumn; they are not edible for humans.

TREE CARE Plant in a large pot, at least 20in (50cm) in diameter, using a peat-free, soil-based potting mix. Water regularly, especially in dry, hot spells, when it's essential to keep the roots moist—move the pot to a shadier spot if possible. The leaves can scorch at the edges in conditions that are too hot, dry, or exposed to wind. Flowering dogwoods require no pruning beyond the removal of dead, damaged, or diseased branches in late winter, although pruning the framework of young trees helps create a balanced shape. Repot trees into fresh potting mix every other year and replace the top inch or so of potting mix in the intervening years (see *p.123*).

The blooms of this dogwood are made up of white petal-like bracts and small green flowers in the center.

ITALIAN CYPRESS *CUPRESSUS SEMPERVIRENS*

HEIGHT & SPREAD 39 × 8ft (12 × 2.5m)
SOIL Well-drained
HARDINESS Zones 8–11

SUN ☼
PRUNING TIME Pruning is not needed
SHAPE 🌲

The Italian cypress can be seen standing sentinel along many Tuscan country roads. Its narrow, upright form makes it ideal for small gardens, whether they are formal or informal, and as it is slow-growing, taking up to 50 years to reach its ultimate height, it can also be easily grown in a container, which will restrict its growth. The dark green foliage is held in sprays on almost vertical branches, which keeps the columnar form neat and compact, narrowing to a pencil-like point at the top. Italian cypresses need little maintenance, apart from regular watering if grown in a pot, and are an easy way to add evergreen structure.

TREE CARE Plant in a pot slightly bigger than the one in which the tree was supplied, using a soil-based, peat-free potting mix mixed with sand in a ratio of 3:1. Repot annually into a slightly larger pot until you reach one of about 20in (50cm) in diameter. This will ensure there is never too much wet soil in the pot. Although the trees are hardy to temperatures of 5°F (−15°C), they will suffer if their roots are soaked, so raise containers on bricks or "pot feet" to ensure they can drain well and place them in a sunny position. The trees require no pruning. Shake heavy snow from the branches before they bend or break under the weight.

Each branch of the Italian cypress grows almost vertically, keeping its narrow shape tight and upright.

ROCKY MOUNTAIN JUNIPER 'BLUE ARROW' *JUNIPERUS SCOPULORUM* 'BLUE ARROW'

HEIGHT & SPREAD 8ft × 20in (2.5 × 0.5m)
SOIL Well-drained
HARDINESS Zones 3–7

SUN ☼
PRUNING TIME Pruning is not needed
SHAPE ▮

Slow-growing rocky mountain juniper is a smaller and hardier alternative to the Italian cypress (see p.79) for an upright, evergreen conifer in a container. As the plants take many years to reach their ultimate height and spread, purchase trees that are the size you require for immediate impact. Their narrow architectural form adds structure and year-round interest to a container garden; they also lend themselves to planting in numbers, placed on each side of doorways or along paths. The foliage is gray-blue, held in dense upright sprays, and pleasantly fragrant. Rocky mountain junipers are low-maintenance and tolerate a wide range of conditions.

TREE CARE Plant in a pot slightly bigger than the one in which the tree was supplied, using a soil-based, peat-free potting mix with added sand in a ratio of 3:1. Raising the pots on bricks or "pot feet" will further aid drainage. Place the pot in a sunny position. Repot every year or two in a slightly larger pot until you reach one of about 20in (50cm) in diameter that is large enough to stabilize the tree. Water regularly, ensuring the potting mix does not become soaked, and feed a liquid fertilizer in summer. The trees require no pruning. Shake heavy snow from the branches before they bend outward or break under the weight.

The steel-blue foliage of 'Blue Arrow' is complemented here by a contemporary metal container.

The flowers of *Magnolia stellata* 'Jane Platt' open deep pink and fade to a blush white.

STAR MAGNOLIA *MAGNOLIA STELLATA*

HEIGHT & SPREAD 5 × 8ft (1.5 × 2.5m)
SOIL Well-drained/moist but well-drained
HARDINESS Zones 4–8

SUN ☼ ☼
PRUNING TIME Summer
SHAPE 🌳

The star magnolia is an ideal choice for a container. Slow-growing and diminutive, it puts on a wonderful show of blossoms in spring before the leaves emerge. Each starlike flower is around 4in (10cm) across and consists of up to 18 narrow, oblong petals. Star magnolias are one of the hardiest of all magnolia species, tolerating a wide range of conditions and winter cold. The plants grow a dense framework of branches on multiple stems and begin flowering even when they are quite young trees. There are a number of varieties of the species available, such as 'Jane Platt', which has deep pink flowers, and 'Royal Star', which can reach up to 13ft (4m) in height and spread and has larger flowers that emerge later in spring than those of the species.

TREE CARE Plant in a large container filled with peat-free, soil-based potting mix and place in a sheltered, bright spot, out of early-morning sun, or dappled shade. Repot annually into a larger pot until it is about 20in (50cm) in diameter. Prune between midsummer and early fall, removing dead, diseased, or damaged wood. To reduce the size or thin the branches on older trees, carry out the changes over a few years. Water regularly and give a liquid feed throughout the spring and summer.

OLIVE TREE *OLEA EUROPAEA*

HEIGHT & SPREAD 26 × 8ft (8 × 2.5m)
SOIL Well-drained
HARDINESS Zones 8–10

SUN ☼
PRUNING TIME Spring
SHAPE 🌳

The olive tree evolved its light, silvery foliage to reflect the heat of the Mediterranean sun and prevent it from losing too much water through its leaves. This adaptation makes it ideal for a hot, sunny yard or patio. Olive trees are also best grown in containers, as they dislike their roots in waterlogged soil over winter. They flower in summer, but fruit worthy of harvesting is unlikely in all but the warmest, longest seasons. Olives are evergreen, adding foliage interest all year round; they have a dense, many-branched crown and a trunk that becomes more characterful with age. These slow-growing trees stay compact for many years.

TREE CARE Olive trees are hardy to 14°F (–10°C) but may die in a cold winter if the roots are in soaked soil. Ideally, move potted trees under cover into an unheated greenhouse or well-lit porch for winter. If this is not possible, protect trees from the coldest spells by covering with them horticultural fleece and wrapping the pot in recycled plastic packaging. Grow olives in three parts peat-free, soil-based potting mix with one part added sand, and water regularly. Give trees a liquid fertilizer in spring and summer. Prune in early to late spring if necessary, removing any dead, diseased, or damaged branches.

Place an olive in a warm, sheltered area and bring indoors over winter in cold regions to protect it from frost.

Kilmarnock willows look most impressive when the branches are left to cascade to the ground.

KILMARNOCK WILLOW *SALIX CAPREA 'KILMARNOCK'*

HEIGHT & SPREAD 8 × 8ft (2.5 × 2.5m)
SOIL Well-drained/moist but well-drained
HARDINESS Zones 4–8

SUN ☼
PRUNING TIME Winter
SHAPE 🌳

The Kilmarnock willow is a dwarf form of weeping willow tree, with pendulous stems growing out of the top of a central stem and cascading down all around it, accumulating more stems the older the tree gets. The branches can be pruned to any length you like: shorten the stems to give your tree a mophead look or allow them to drape elegantly down to the ground. In early spring the branches bear yellow catkins, which open from furry gray buds; these are an excellent source of protein-rich pollen for bumblebees and bees. The leaves are narrow and elongated, mid-green in color, and emerge after the catkins.

TREE CARE Plant in soil-based, peat-free potting mix. If your tree is small, you can transfer it into a larger pot size each year, but more substantial specimens should be given containers that offer plenty of space for the roots to expand. The trees will fare best in an open, sunny position. Water them regularly, since willows are thirsty plants, and give them a liquid fertilizer throughout the spring and summer. Kilmarnock willows benefit from annual pruning to keep them in shape and prevent congested growth. In late winter, thin out the stems to form an open, umbrella shape, removing old stems first, and shorten those remaining by half their length.

CITRUS SPECIES *CITRUS* SPECIES

HEIGHT & SPREAD Up to 20 x 8ft (6 x 2.5m)
SOIL Moist but well-drained
HARDINESS Zones 9–11

SUN ☼
PRUNING TIME Early spring
SHAPE 🌳

The citrus family includes lemons, oranges, limes, grapefruit, and kumquats as well as makrut lime, which is used for its aromatic leaves. They are all grown in the same way, and form similar trees, with glossy mid-green foliage and spiny branches. Their blossoms have a delectable fragrance; they can be in fruit and flower all year round, and at the same time. Most of the fruits are simply sold under their common names, but good varieties to look out for are the Meyer lemon (*C. x meyeri*), a compact and relatively hardy tree bearing delicious fruit, and *C. aurantiifolia* 'Tahiti' (syn. 'Persian'), a relatively small lime tree.

TREE CARE Citrus trees cannot tolerate low temperatures below freezing, nor wet conditions. They are therefore best grown in containers that can be moved in the fall to a heated greenhouse or cool porch (they also do not like centrally heated homes). In summer they will be very happy in a sunny, sheltered area, such as a patio. Aim to keep them no colder than 57°F (14°C) at all times and at daytime temperatures of about 68–77°F (20–25°C) in summer. Plant in a pot at least 20in (50cm) in diameter and use a soil-based, peat-free potting mix. Prune in early spring to shape the tree and again in summer to control the size if needed.

An orange tree in a pot is easily moved under cover during the cold winter months.

Pick quince before the first frosts of winter and ripen further indoors, where you can enjoy their fragrance.

QUINCE 'CHAMPION' *CYDONIA OBLONGA* 'CHAMPION'

HEIGHT & SPREAD Up to 8 x 5ft (2.5 x 1.5m)
SOIL Moist but well-drained
HARDINESS Zones 4–9

SUN ☼
PRUNING TIME Winter
SHAPE 🌳

Quince are beautiful fruit trees, with large dark green leaves and large blush-pink blossoms opening from pink buds in spring. They bear pear-shaped fruit in late autumn as the leaves turn yellow and fall. The developing fruitlets are pale green and covered in a downy fluff. As they ripen, they turn bright yellow, and although in a temperate climate they rarely ripen fully on the tree, they will continue to ripen when taken indoors, perfuming the room with their floral fragrance. 'Champion' is a compact variety that fruits from a young age, producing a regular crop. Even when ripe, quince can be a little pithy to eat raw, but cooked with apple in a pie or crumble or made into membrillo (a sliceable quince jelly), they are delicious.

TREE CARE 'Champion' tolerates dry soils well but will do best in a moist but well-drained soil and a sheltered, sunny spot, which will help protect its spring blossom from frost damage. Formative pruning will help establish an open framework shaped like a goblet. Water young trees as they establish and mature trees during long dry periods when they are flowering and fruiting. Mature trees need little maintenance beyond an annual prune in winter to remove any dead, diseased, or badly placed branches.

APPLE *MALUS DOMESTICA*

Apple trees are a pretty sight in the garden as well as being productive. They are also very straightforward to grow, requiring only a little pruning each year to keep them healthy. They can be pruned to fit into almost any space and trained against vertical surfaces or into different shapes, making them an extremely flexible choice of fruit tree for gardens of all sizes.

HEIGHT & SPREAD up to 13 × 13ft (4 × 4m)
SOIL Moist but well-drained
HARDINESS Zones 4–8
SUN ☼
PRUNING TIME Winter/summer
SHAPE 🌳 🪴 ❘

Most apples, regardless of rootstock or variety, are similar in appearance: mid- to deep green ovate leaves (yellow in the fall) and white or blush-pink blossoms in early spring, opening from pink and white buds.

ROOTSTOCKS

All apple varieties are grafted (joined) onto a rootstock of known vigor. By choosing an appropriate rootstock, you can know the approximate ultimate size of the tree. For small yards and trained trees, choose a dwarfing rootstock, such as M27 (very dwarfing, suitable for cordons); M9 (dwarfing,

Perfectly ripe apples, picked in season, are all the more delicious when they are homegrown.

Training an apple as an espalier against a wall saves space and adds visual interest throughout the seasons.

use for cordons and espaliers); or M26 (semi-dwarfing, for trained or freestanding fruit trees). (*See also p.31.*)

VARIETIES

There are hundreds of apple varieties to choose from, divided into dessert (eating) apples and cooking apples, with some that can be used for both purposes. Their flavor profiles range from juicy and sweet to nutty and crisp, and everything in between. An 'apple day' or fall garden show can be a chance to try different varieties before you buy a tree, or you can peruse the catalogs of fruit tree nurseries. Unless there are apple trees in your area, you will need

ALSO TRY

Apple trees are especially suitable for training onto horizontal wires fixed to walls and fences, and grown in this way, they take up very little space and add architectural interest to the yard. The simplest form is an oblique cordon, a single stem with short fruiting branches, tied at a 45° angle to the ground (see pp. 36–37 on planting a cordon), but you could also try an espalier, as pictured. Use trees on dwarfing rootstocks and prune both in winter to establish the framework and in summer to reduce the excess foliage growth.

two trees in the same pollination group (flowering at the same time) to ensure good harvests.

TREE CARE Apple trees fruit best in a sunny position and a moist but well-drained soil. Water young trees and those grown in containers regularly, and water mature trees in very dry spells, especially when flowering and fruiting. Prune trees to establish a strong framework in the first few years, then continue to prune every winter to maintain them, taking out dead or diseased branches, removing crossing branches, and shortening new growth.

CHERRY *PRUNUS AVIUM* 'LAPINS'

HEIGHT & SPREAD up to 13 x 13ft (4 x 4m)
SOIL Moist but well-drained
HARDINESS Zones 5–8

SUN ☼
PRUNING TIME Summer
SHAPE 🌳

This cherry tree will provide heavy crops of fruit to pick in midsummer. It is self-fertile, so it is ideal if you have room for only one tree. The cherries are dark red, large, sweet, and juicy and are resistant to splitting as they ripen. A strong, upright tree, it can be planted freestanding or trained against a warm wall; the ultimate size depends upon the rootstock used (*see p.31*). In spring, the branches are covered in white blossoms, and during the fall the foliage turns a brilliant red-orange. 'Lapins' is sometimes sold as 'Cherokee' or 'Lapins Cherokee'. For a smaller cherry tree that can even be grown in containers, try *Prunus avium* 'Celeste'.

TREE CARE Cherry trees will fruit best in a warm, sheltered, and sunny spot, with a rich soil. Young trees will need watering regularly as their roots establish, and mature trees will also benefit from watering during dry spells in spring and summer as they blossom and the fruit develops. Prune in summer to prevent trees contracting diseases such as silver leaf and bacterial canker, taking out dead, diseased, and damaged branches and shortening or removing any that are crossing or crowding the overall framework. Aim for an open goblet or vase shape with a balanced number of branches so that air and light can access the center of the crown.

Ripe cherries will be a deep red; pick them by gently detaching their stalks from the branch.

PLUM *PRUNUS DOMESTICA* 'VICTORIA'

HEIGHT & SPREAD up to 13 x 13ft (4 x 4m)
SOIL Well-drained/moist but well-drained
HARDINESS Zones 4–9

SUN ☼
PRUNING TIME Summer
SHAPE 🌳

Victoria plums are easily available in stores, but nothing compares with the taste of fruit eaten straight from the tree.

'Victoria' is the most popular plum variety in the world, and with good reason. It is self-fertile, so it will fruit well even if you only have one tree. It is also versatile—the fruit can be eaten fresh as dessert plums or used for culinary purposes in puddings, jam, and more. The stones come away from the flesh easily ("freestone"). The tree will tolerate dry soils and produces white blossoms in spring, followed by reliably heavy crops of red-purple fruit with yellow flesh in late summer and early autumn. The tree's ultimate size depends on which rootstock is used (*see p.31*); for a smaller tree, choose a dwarfing rootstock, such as 'Pixy'.

TREE CARE Plant in a sunny, sheltered location as a freestanding tree or train it against a warm wall, which will help the fruit ripen. It will grow well in most soils, provided they are not waterlogged over winter. Water a young tree regularly as its roots establish; water a mature tree in long dry spells, especially during flowering and fruiting. Prune in midsummer or after harvest, taking out dead, damaged, or diseased wood, and also any branches crossing the center of the crown or crowding better-placed branches. Maintain the crown in an open-centered goblet shape so that light and air can penetrate to keep it healthy and ripen the fruit.

PEACH *PRUNUS PERSICA*

HEIGHT & SPREAD up to 13 × 13ft (4 × 4m)
SOIL Moist but well-drained
HARDINESS Zones 4–9

SUN ☼
PRUNING TIME Spring/summer
SHAPE 🌳

Peaches are ideal candidates for training onto a wall, where they take up hardly any space. They fruit in summer, but their most ornamental feature is the deep pink blossom, borne on bare branches. The leaves are mid-green and large, and the baby fruits are delightfully fuzzy and tactile. There are several choices that are more suited to cooler temperate climates, such as heritage varieties 'Peregrine' and 'Rochester' that fruit in midsummer, or 'Avalon Pride', with ripe fruit in late summer.

TREE CARE Peach trees flower very early in spring, when the blossoms are susceptible to damage by frost.

However, if you plant them in a warm, sheltered, and sunny spot and give them some protection, you should still achieve a harvest. Covering the tree with horticultural fleece is a good way to protect it from frost on cold nights, which is easier to do on wall-trained trees than freestanding ones. Although the trees are self-fertile, they will benefit from hand-pollination—there are few insects around in early spring to do the job. Use a small paintbrush to brush the centers of the flowers on a sunny afternoon. Repeat a few days later. Prune in spring to maintain an open-centered, goblet-shaped crown for freestanding trees, removing misplaced or diseased branches.

A homegrown, fully ripe peach is more flavorful than store-bought fruits, which are usually harvested unripe.

Pear trees will fruit best in a warm, sunny spot where their blossoms are less likely to be damaged by frost.

PEAR *PYRUS COMMUNIS*

HEIGHT & SPREAD up to 13 × 13ft (4 × 4m)
SOIL Well-drained/moist but well-drained
HARDINESS Zones 5–9

SUN ☼
PRUNING TIME Winter
SHAPE 🌳

Pears naturally hold their branches relatively upright, so even freestanding trees take up little space. They can also be trained onto a wall as a cordon or espalier, where they will still provide a generous harvest. Their ultimate size depends on the rootstock. The spring blossoms are white, emerging at the same time as the glossy, light green leaves; the autumn foliage is a rich, buttery yellow. Pears are either dessert or culinary varieties, and most need to be planted with a compatible variety for good pollination. Alternatively, you could plant a "family tree," bred to bear several compatible pear varieties on one tree. Juicy dessert pears to plant together are 'Williams' Bon Chrétién' and 'Concorde', which are both compact trees. 'Obelisk', a columnar dwarf variety, will also match well with either of those, as will reliable cropper 'Conference'.

TREE CARE Plant pears in a sheltered, sunny location, whether as freestanding trees or trained against a wall. They grow well in most soils but will need watering when young and during long dry spells, especially when flowering and fruiting. Prune in winter to remove damaged, diseased, or dead wood, take out any crossing or overcrowded branches—an open goblet shape is the aim—and shorten new shoots by around half.

Rowan trees (*Sorbus*) put on a dual performance of blazing foliage colors and red, pink, or white berries to decorate an autumn yard.

TREES FOR SEASONAL INTEREST

Few plants can compete with the show-stopping beauty of an apple or cherry tree decked with spring blossoms or laden with the fruits that follow. Other trees, such as rowans and acers, wait until winter is almost upon us before putting on their finest performance, when the leaves turn from cool greens to shimmering hues of red, orange, and gold. The katsura tree takes this seasonal gift to another level, filling the air with a sweet cotton candy scent as the foliage colors and then falls.

GREY ALDER 'AUREA' *ALNUS INCANA* 'AUREA'

HEIGHT & SPREAD 26 × 13ft (8 × 4m)
SOIL Well-drained/moist but well-drained
HARDINESS Zones 2–6

SUN ☼
PRUNING TIME Winter
SHAPE 🌲

The golden hues of the gray alder 'Aurea' are a colorful foil for the reddish male catkins in spring.

'Aurea' is a striking deciduous tree that is ideal for gardens with problematic soil conditions, such as being waterlogged or, conversely, very dry. It has a conical shape, and grows slowly, forming a smaller tree than the species. The glossy bark is a golden-orange color that stands out beautifully in winter and early spring, when it contrasts strikingly with the catkins as they emerge on the bare branches. The reddish or coral-pink male catkins can be up to 4in (10cm) long and are held on the tree into summer. Female catkins are shorter, green, and ripen once pollinated into hard, dark brown, conelike seed pods that persist on the tree into winter; the seeds are useful winter food for birds such as siskins. The golden-green leaves are ovate, with serrated edges.

TREE CARE Alders can be planted in any garden soil, including wet, and they also thrive in windy sites. Newly planted trees will need watering regularly while their roots establish in the soil. The gray alder 'Aurea' is a low-maintenance tree and will need pruning only if there are damaged, dead, or diseased branches that need removing. Carry this out in winter while the tree is dormant, taking out any other branches that are spoiling the overall shape of the crown at the same time.

The blossom of 'Robin Hill' emerges early in spring, providing essential nectar and pollen for insects.

JUNEBERRY 'ROBIN HILL' *AMELANCHIER ARBOREA* 'ROBIN HILL'

HEIGHT & SPREAD 26 × 13ft (8 × 4m)
SOIL Moist but well-drained
HARDINESS Zones 4–8

SUN ☼ ☼
PRUNING TIME Winter
SHAPE 🪵

'Robin Hill' is an upright form of *Amelanchier* that grows on a single trunk, making it the most treelike of the genus—others form multi-stemmed or shrubby trees. The branches are held almost erect into a narrow crown at first, although they spread outward slightly with age. In spring, pink buds open into pale pink, star-shaped, single flowers with narrow petals; although they are individually small, they are borne in profusion and create a spectacular effect. The bronzed young foliage contrasts beautifully with the flowers and then matures to an emerald green for summer. In autumn, the leaves turn brilliant shades of red and orange.

Small, dark purple, edible berries are produced in summer, but you may want to leave them as a feast for the birds, as 'Robin Hill' does not produce as many berries as other *Amelanchier* species.

TREE CARE Juneberry trees prefer moist, neutral to acidic soils and won't grow well in alkaline (limy) conditions (see pp.26–27). 'Robin Hill' will tolerate exposure to wind, and full sun or partial shade. Water young trees regularly until their roots are established. Prune in winter only if necessary to remove any dead, broken, or diseased branches; formative pruning to take out crossing shoots may be needed at the same time.

BIRCH 'FASCINATION' *BETULA* 'FASCINATION'

HEIGHT & SPREAD 33 × 13ft (10 × 4m)
SOIL Well-drained/moist but well-drained
HARDINESS Zones 5–8

SUN ☼ ☼
PRUNING TIME Winter
SHAPE ▲

'Fascination' is a neat, elegant tree with year-round interest. Its branches are held relatively upright, giving its crown a slender pyramidal or conical habit. The bark is white with a pale orange hue, but as it peels, it reveals a deeper orange-brown underside, emphasized when the loose curls catch the low sun in early spring and winter. Catkins are produced in abundance in spring; the male catkins are the most striking, at around 4in (10cm) or more long, initially bright yellow but then fading to brown as they age. The foliage emerges while the catkins are still on the tree, at first bright green then maturing to dark green and turning buttercup yellow during the fall. The leaves are large, ovate with narrowly pointed tips and serrated edges.

TREE CARE 'Fascination' can be planted in a wide range of soils and situations. Young trees will need regular watering while their roots establish. Mature trees should need little maintenance except for pruning out any dead or damaged branches, which can be done in winter. It is possible to keep the trunk bright by removing larger pieces of the old bark that are just hanging on and washing the trunk with very dilute soapy water, but don't be tempted to peel off the bark yourself, as this can damage the tree.

The white and orange-brown bark of birch 'Fascination' is an attractive feature all year round.

HONEY LOCUST 'SUNBURST' *GLEDITSIA TRIACANTHOS* F. *INERMIS* 'SUNBURST'

HEIGHT & SPREAD Up to 26 × 13ft (8 × 4m)
SOIL Well-drained/moist but well-drained
HARDINESS Zones 3–9

SUN ☼
PRUNING TIME Winter
SHAPE ▯ ●

The foliage of 'Sunburst' is especially vibrant during the spring, when it is golden-yellow until summer.

'Sunburst' is a small to medium-sized tree grown for its eye-catching deciduous foliage. It has a broadly columnar to rounded crown, becoming more spreading with age, but a light and airy branch structure that casts little shade beneath it. In spring, the leaves emerge a vibrant yellow, becoming lime green in summer and then turning golden yellow in the fall. They are composed of narrow, lance-shaped leaflets held in opposite pairs along the stalk. Unlike other *Gleditsia* species, 'Sunburst' does not have thorny branches; the bark is attractive, with narrow dark and lighter stripes. It does not produce showy blossom, but inconspicuous small green flowers may be seen in spring, followed by flat seed pods that hang from the branches into winter.

TREE CARE 'Sunburst' is best planted in a spot where the sun will highlight the spring foliage; it will stand out even better if it has a dark background, such as evergreen conifers or a dark fence or wall. It tolerates some exposure and air pollution and also grows well in dry soils; it does not like being waterlogged, but a newly planted tree will need to be watered regularly while its roots establish. Relatively fast-growing, it needs pruning only to remove damaged, dead, or diseased branches in winter.

The Carolina silverbell's white flowers are very attractive to pollinators such as bees during the spring.

CAROLINA SILVERBELL *HALESIA CAROLINA*

HEIGHT & SPREAD 30 × 20ft (9 × 6m)
SOIL Moist but well-drained
HARDINESS Zones 4–8

SUN ☼ ☼
PRUNING TIME Winter
SHAPE 🌳

The Carolina silverbell is so named for its spring display of bell-shaped flowers, which are useful for pollinating insects such as bumblebees. It has a rounded, spreading crown and can be grown either as a multi-stemmed tree or with a broad crown on a short single trunk. It's an architectural specimen for the back of a border or a woodland-style garden, or grow it as a stand-alone tree. The flowers emerge just before the leaves, growing in clusters beneath the branches. The petals are pure white, forming a bell shape about 1in (2.5cm) across. The deciduous leaves are small and ovate, with a finely toothed edge; they are mid-green through spring and summer, turning slightly yellow in fall but lacking significant color. Pale green, four-winged fruits, popular with wildlife, are produced in autumn.

TREE CARE This tree likes a rich, moist soil with a neutral to acidic pH (see *pp.26–27*); if the soil is too alkaline, the leaves may take on a yellow hue (known as chlorosis). It will grow well in partial or dappled shade as well as full sun. Young trees will need regular watering while their roots establish. Mature trees are low-maintenance: simply prune out dead, diseased, or crossing stems and branches while the tree is dormant in winter.

MAGNOLIA 'CAERHAYS SURPRISE' *MAGNOLIA* 'CAERHAYS SURPRISE'

HEIGHT & SPREAD 16 × 16ft (5 × 5m)
SOIL Moist but well-drained
HARDINESS Zones 5–9

SUN ☼ ☼
PRUNING TIME Summer
SHAPE 🌳

'Caerhays Surprise' is a small deciduous tree that is an elegant choice for spring color. The large, goblet-shaped flowers emerge in mid- to late spring and slowly reflex into a more cup-and-saucer shape about 8in (20cm) across. The petals are lilac on the inside with a magenta flush to the base and outside, paling as they mature; each flower has 9–12 long petals. This plant flowers prolifically and from a relatively young age for a magnolia, holding its flowers on the branches for several weeks. Its leaves are about 8in (20cm) long, with smooth edges; they are mid-green from spring to autumn, slightly brighter when they initially unfurl but with no distinct fall color.

TREE CARE Although the branch structure of magnolias is hardy, to thrive they need a sheltered position protected from harsh winds and the worst of the winter cold, which will potentially damage the spring flowers. 'Caerhays Surprise' prefers a neutral or acidic soil (see *pp.26–27*). Prune between midsummer and early fall if it is necessary to remove any dead, diseased, or damaged wood. To reduce the size or thin the branches on older trees, carry out the changes over a few years rather than all at once to avoid stressing the tree. Water newly planted and young trees regularly, especially in dry spells, while the roots are establishing.

The deep pink flowers of 'Caerhays Surprise' make a change from the pastel shades of other spring blossoms.

The flowers of 'Brozzonii' open on bare branches but are still in bloom when the leaves start to open.

SAUCER MAGNOLIA 'BROZZONII' *MAGNOLIA x SOULANGEANA* 'BROZZONII'

HEIGHT & SPREAD 16 x 13ft (5 x 4m)
SOIL Moist but well-drained
HARDINESS Zones 5–9

SUN ☼ ☀
PRUNING TIME Summer
SHAPE 🌳

'Brozzonii' is a deciduous magnolia that has the typically large, spreading crown of the species; it can be grown on a short single trunk or as a multi-stemmed tree. As it blooms later than other saucer magnolias, its flowers are less susceptible to spring frosts. They open on bare branches in late spring, forming a goblet shape before gradually opening into the roughly 8in (20cm) cup-and-saucer form that gives the species its name. The petals are white, with a lilac blush to the base that fades as the flowers age. Although bright green when they unfurl, the large, leathery leaves mature to a glossy dark green; they are ovate with a slight point at the tip.

TREE CARE Plant in a neutral or acidic, moist, and rich soil (see pp.26–27) in a sheltered position. Magnolia trees are hardy, but their spring flowers need protection from frost and cold winds, or they will brown and fall prematurely. If it is necessary to remove any dead, diseased, or damaged wood, prune them between midsummer and early fall. Older trees can be reduced in size or have their branches thinned if required, but do this pruning in stages over a few years rather than all at once to avoid stressing the tree. Newly planted and young trees will need regular watering while the roots are establishing, especially in dry spells.

CRAB APPLE 'PINK PERFECTION' *MALUS* 'PINK PERFECTION'

HEIGHT & SPREAD 5 x 3m (16 x 10ft)
SOIL Moist but well-drained
HARDINESS Zones 3–8

SUN ☼ ☀
PRUNING TIME Winter
SHAPE 🌳

Crab apple 'Pink Perfection' forms a compact, upright tree with a slightly spreading crown, ideal in smaller yards or more formal planting schemes. In spring, abundant blush-pink flowers open from dark pink buds that are set off well by the lime-green color of the juvenile leaves that unfurl soon afterward. Unusually for a crab apple, the flowers are semi-double, but they are held wide open and so are popular with insects. Once pollinated, the tree develops small green fruits about the size of a cherry, which ripen to red in the fall. These are edible, if too tart to eat raw, and can be picked to make crab apple jelly or other preserves; alternatively, leave them on the tree, where they will provide winter food for birds and other wildlife.

TREE CARE This tree grows well in most soils. It is hardy enough to handle some exposure to winds, but do not plant it in a frost pocket or a north- or east-facing aspect, as spring frosts and cold winds may damage the blossoms. Water young trees regularly. Create a balanced framework with formative pruning, but after that, crab apples need only minimal or no pruning. In winter, while the tree is dormant, take out any broken, diseased, or dead branches and any that are crossing or badly placed.

The rosy-pink buds of 'Pink Perfection' open into an abundant display of blush-pink and white blossoms.

TORINGO CRAB APPLE 'SCARLETT' *MALUS TORINGO* 'SCARLETT'

HEIGHT & SPREAD 8 × 10ft (2.5 × 3m)
SOIL Moist but well-drained
HARDINESS Zones 3–8

SUN ☼ ◐
PRUNING TIME Winter
SHAPE 🌳

'Scarlett' is a low-growing, spreading deciduous tree, with arching branches that add architectural structure even in winter. This also makes it a useful choice for screening. In spring, it puts on a double display of colorful blossoms and juvenile foliage: the unfurling leaves are a deep, bronzed-purple color, complementing the clusters of cerise flowers. They turn a glossy, dark green color for summer, then take on shades of coppery red and yellow for fall; they remain on the tree much later in the season than other crab apples. The apples that develop over summer ripen to purple and are held on the tree through autumn and into winter, providing food for birds.

TREE CARE Grow 'Scarlett' in a fertile, moist, but well-drained soil in full sun or partial shade. Spring frosts and cold winds can damage the spring blossoms, so a sheltered spot in a south- or west-facing position is ideal, although the branch framework is fully hardy. Water newly planted trees regularly while their roots are establishing. Toringo crab apples need minimal or no pruning, although some formative pruning can help create a balanced framework of branches. On mature trees, remove only broken, dead, and diseased branches and any that are crossing or misaligned. Prune in winter while the tree is dormant.

The profuse spring blossom and fruits combined make 'Scarlett' an excellent tree for wildlife.

CHERRY 'ACCOLADE' *PRUNUS* 'ACCOLADE'

HEIGHT & SPREAD Up to 26 × 13ft (8 × 4m)
SOIL Well-drained/moist but well-drained
HARDINESS Zones 6–8

SUN ☼
PRUNING TIME Summer
SHAPE 🌳

Ornamental cherries are a reliable choice for spring color, and 'Accolade' is an excellent pink-flowered variety. The blossoms cover the bare branches in early to mid-spring: opening from dark pink buds, the pale pink, double flowers are around 1½in (4cm) wide and hang in clusters. The leaves are ovate and thin, with a serrated edge. Bright green in spring, they darken slightly as they mature, turning beautiful shades of red, orange, and purple in autumn before they fall. 'Accolade' has a rounded, spreading habit. Whether you buy a single- or multi-stemmed form, its network of dark stems will provide ornamental interest even in the depths of winter.

TREE CARE For the best spring blossoms and fall color, plant in a sunny and ideally sheltered position. Like many other ornamental cherries, it is also tolerant of urban air pollution. They are not too fussy about soil type, but ensure that their roots do not sit in waterlogged conditions. Water young trees regularly for at least two years after planting while their roots establish, especially during dry spells. Prune in summer, removing only dead, diseased, or damaged branches; formative pruning and keeping a balanced framework can be done at the same time by taking out any misplaced branches if necessary.

Clouds of pink blossom make 'Accolade' a striking sight in spring, while the foliage provides autumn color.

CHERRY 'SHIROFUGEN' *PRUNUS* 'SHIROFUGEN'

HEIGHT & SPREAD 20 × 20ft (6 × 6m)
SOIL Well-drained/moist but well-drained
HARDINESS Zones 6–8

SUN ☀
PRUNING TIME Summer
SHAPE 🌳

Cherry 'Shirofugen' is excellent for adding spring color and height to a formal garden.

'Shirofugen' is a small to medium ornamental cherry with a wide, spreading, and flattened crown that is useful where a taller tree might block out too much light. Clusters of ruffled double flowers open in mid-spring and are held on the tree for about a month, depending on the weather. They are 2in (5cm) wide, pink in bud, opening to reveal white petals that then turn lilac in color. The young foliage is a dark, coppery-purple color that complements the blossom beautifully. The ovate leaves have a slightly toothed edge and pointed tip. They fade to a fresh green for summer and then turn bright golden-orange in autumn before falling.

TREE CARE Cherry 'Shirofugen' will grow well in most gardens, although it will flower best in a sunny and sheltered position; it is not fussy about soil type and will also tolerate urban air pollution. Water newly planted trees while their roots are establishing in the soil, especially during dry spells. This is a low-maintenance tree that needs little regular pruning. Just remove dead, diseased, damaged, or crossing branches and carry out formative pruning to create a balanced framework in summer. Cutting at this time of year helps reduce the risk of the tree developing silver leaf disease, to which cherries are prone.

The clusters of white blossom on cherry 'Shirotae' resemble pompoms on the bare branches.

CHERRY 'SHIROTAE' *PRUNUS* 'SHIROTAE'

HEIGHT & SPREAD Up to 13 × 16ft (4 × 5m)
SOIL Well-drained/moist but well-drained
HARDINESS Zones 6–8

SUN ☀
PRUNING TIME Summer
SHAPE 🌳

Cherry 'Shirotae' is a small, spreading tree, ultimately wider than it is tall, with young branches that droop at the ends. Larger branches on mature trees add gnarled architectural interest, reaching almost to the ground in places; the trees look especially effective underplanted with spring bulbs. The blossom, held in clusters on bare branches, is pure white, the double flowers about 2in (5cm) across, with an almond scent. The foliage emerges a fresh, bright green; darkens slightly for summer; and turns vivid reds and oranges in autumn. 'Shirotae' is also known as the Mount Fuji cherry because the tree in blossom resembles the mountain's snow-capped peak.

TREE CARE 'Shirotae' will grow well in most soils other than wet, but plant it in a sunny and sheltered position for the best spring blossoms and fall color. It tolerates urban air pollution. Water young trees regularly for at least two years after planting while their roots establish, especially during dry spells. 'Shirotae' only needs dead, diseased, or damaged branches to be removed each year, but formative pruning to keep a balanced framework can be done at the same time. Pruning in summer helps prevent the tree from contracting silver leaf disease because the fungal spores are less prevalent at this time of year.

Ornamental cherries such as 'Ukon' can be planted together in a line to make a spring avenue.

CHERRY 'UKON' *PRUNUS* 'UKON'

HEIGHT & SPREAD Up to 26 × 39ft (8 × 12m)
SOIL Well-drained/moist but well-drained
HARDINESS Zones 6–8

SUN ☀
PRUNING TIME Summer
SHAPE 🌳

The ornamental cherry 'Ukon' erupts into a profuse display of pale yellow blossoms on its bare branches in spring, while the new foliage that unfurls soon afterward complements the flowers with its deep, coppery-brown tones. The flowers are semi-double, 2in (5cm) across, and hang in clusters; occasionally the petals take on a pink blush. The ovate, toothed leaves are green in summer, followed by vibrant fall color in shades of purple, red, and copper. The tree has a spreading, open crown that doesn't readily branch and will ultimately be wider than it is tall. The glossy yellow-brown bark adds ornamental interest even in winter.

TREE CARE For the best spring blossoms and fall color, plant 'Ukon' in a sunny and relatively sheltered position. Ornamental cherries will grow well in most garden soils, aside from wet types, since they dislike waterlogged conditions. Water newly planted trees regularly for the first two years while their roots establish, especially during dry spells. Prune in summer to remove dead, diseased, or damaged branches; to keep a balanced framework, take out any misplaced branches and shorten new growth by half on a few of the branches. Cutting at this time of year helps reduce the risk of silver leaf disease, to which cherries are prone.

LITTLE EPAULETTE TREE *PTEROSTYRAX CORYMBOSA*

HEIGHT & SPREAD 16 × 13ft (5 × 4m)
SOIL Well-drained
HARDINESS Zones 5–9

SUN ☀ ☀
PRUNING TIME Winter
SHAPE 🌳 🌳

A small, deciduous tree with a crown that spreads as it matures, the little epaulette tree is an excellent choice for a spring garden. The leaves emerge before the flowers: a fresh, yellowy-green in color, they are ovate with a distinct point at the tip, serrated edges, fine indentations along the veins, and a slight upward fold along the central midrib. In late spring the flowers are borne on panicles (a stalk holding clusters of flowers) up to 5in (12cm) long. Creamy-white and fragrant, they are bell-shaped and about ¾in (2cm) long, narrow at first but opening wider as they mature, with the prominent white stamens dangling below the petals. In fall the foliage turns yellow, with more orange and red tones if the soil is particularly acidic, and hairy, brown, five-ribbed fruits also appear. The aromatic bark peels attractively.

TREE CARE Plant this tree in fertile, well-drained soil with a neutral or acidic pH (see pp.26–27). It will do best in a south- or west-facing spot, sheltered from strong winds, but will not thrive in soil that is waterlogged in winter. Water young plants regularly until their roots are established. The tree should need little, if any, pruning. If necessary, remove damaged, dead, diseased, or badly placed branches in late winter.

The little epaulette tree is so called for the way in which the stamens frill out below the petals.

The pendulous willow-leaved pear is an elegant choice for a small yard, adding structure even in winter.

PENDULOUS WILLOW-LEAVED PEAR *PYRUS SALICIFOLIA* 'PENDULA'

HEIGHT & SPREAD 20 x 20ft (6 x 6m)
SOIL Well-drained/moist but well-drained
HARDINESS Zones 4–8

SUN ☀
PRUNING TIME Winter
SHAPE 🌳

This tree is notable for its weeping crown of silvery deciduous foliage. It is slow-growing, initially mopheaded with the branches cascading lower to the ground as it ages, adding architectural structure to the garden even in winter. Its blossoms are white, each flower a bowl shape of five petals, and emerges at the same time as the new leaves. These are frosted gray-green on the upper surface and silvery with a downy fuzz on the underside. Long and narrow, they hang down from the branch, giving a waterfall effect. In autumn, they take on a green-bronze appearance before falling. The flowers are popular with pollinating insects, while the brownish-green fruits that follow in the fall are useful food stores for birds and other wildlife at the onset of winter.

TREE CARE This is a hardy tree, tolerant of any aspect and some exposure, although the blossoms will fare best in a sheltered spot away from cold winds and spring frosts. A newly planted tree will need regular watering while the roots establish. Little to no pruning is needed; if it is necessary, carry it out while the tree is dormant in winter, removing any damaged, dead, and diseased branches. You can also thin the branches or shorten them if they are too close to the ground.

LILAC 'KATHERINE HAVEMEYER' *SYRINGA VULGARIS* 'KATHERINE HAVEMEYER'

HEIGHT & SPREAD Up to 13 x 13ft (4 x 4m)
SOIL Well-drained/moist but well-drained
HARDINESS Zones 6–8

SUN ☀
PRUNING TIME Winter
SHAPE 🌳

'Katherine Havemeyer' is a small deciduous tree that can be grown on a short trunk or as a multi-stemmed specimen. It is ultimately as wide as it is tall, its upright branches becoming more spreading with age. The leaves are ovate to heart-shaped, up to 4in (10cm) long, and a fresh tone of grass green; they have no noteworthy fall color. In late spring, the panicles (stalks) of small, dark purple flower buds become more congested, compact, and cone-shaped as the flowers open, held upright or slightly drooping on the top of the branches. Opening lavender blue or mauve, they fade to a lilac-pink color, lasting 3–4 weeks, depending on weather conditions. The blooms of this cultivar are especially fragrant and are popular with bees and butterflies.

TREE CARE Plant this tree in an alkaline or neutral soil (see pp.26–27). It flowers best in a sunny spot but will be happy in any position, and it will also tolerate some exposure in windy locations. Young trees will need regular watering while their roots establish. Remove any damaged, dead, or diseased branches in late winter if necessary. Avoid any other pruning on young trees where possible. To rejuvenate older specimens or to reduce their size, prune back to a stumpy framework in late winter.

The dark buds and paler petals of 'Katherine Havemeyer' give the blossom a two-tone effect.

RED CAPPADOCIAN MAPLE *ACER CAPPADOCICUM* 'RUBRUM'

HEIGHT & SPREAD 26 × 13ft (8 × 4m)
SOIL Well-drained/moist but well-drained
HARDINESS Zones 5–7

SUN ☀ ☀
PRUNING TIME Winter
SHAPE 🌳

The red Cappadocian maple is red in spring rather than fall, but it is a colorful specimen all year round. It is slow-growing and will eventually form a medium-sized tree with a rounded crown. In spring, the deciduous foliage emerges bright crimson or scarlet. As summer approaches, the five-lobed leaves turn green from the center first, pushing the red coloration out to the leaf margins. In the fall they turn a bright, buttery yellow; because they are thin, their color is especially enhanced when the low autumn sun shines through them. They resist scorch well. Young shoots have reddish-brown bark, while older branches develop vertical striations in green and white. Insignificant yellow flowers are produced on this tree in spring.

TREE CARE Grow the red Cappadocian maple in a sheltered spot, out of cold winds. It will grow well in most gardens but prefers moist, well-drained soil. Water newly planted trees regularly while their roots establish. Mature trees need little or no maintenance. If it is necessary to remove any damaged, dead, or diseased branches, carry this out in winter while the tree is dormant. Badly placed branches can be taken out at the same time to balance the crown's framework, if desired.

The leaves of the red Cappadocian maple turn from red in spring to green in summer, then finally yellow in autumn.

The freeman maple 'Autumn Blaze' provides a reliable display of color when planted in a sunny location.

FREEMAN MAPLE 'AUTUMN BLAZE' *ACER* X *FREEMANII* 'AUTUMN BLAZE'

HEIGHT & SPREAD 33 × 20ft (10 × 6m)
SOIL Well-drained/moist but well-drained
HARDINESS Zones 3–8

SUN ☀ ☀
PRUNING TIME Winter
SHAPE 🌳

'Autumn Blaze' is also known as 'Jeffersred', but it is the former name that best describes its fall color: the leaves do seem to be on fire, in intense shades of red and orange. It grows quickly, forming an upright shape with an oval crown. In spring, the deciduous foliage emerges emerald green, looking all the fresher for the contrast with the smooth silvery-gray bark, darkening a little in summer before turning red, orange, and plum for autumn. The five-lobed leaves are deeply indented and toothed, with a silvery shimmer to the underside. Winged seeds are sometimes seen, following the insignificant flowers in spring.

TREE CARE While some maples will put on better displays of fall color in more acidic soils or sheltered locations, 'Autumn Blaze' is well-suited to a cooler climate and will perform well in any soil type or pH (see pp.26–27). Plant it in a sheltered location in full sun or partial shade. Young trees will need watering regularly while their roots establish. Remove damaged, dead, or diseased branches on mature trees if necessary, but no further pruning should be required. Should there be any badly placed branches in the crown's framework, they can be taken out at the same time. Carry out all pruning in winter while the tree is dormant.

SHAGBARK HICKORY *CARYA OVATA*

HEIGHT & SPREAD up to 20 × 15m (66 × 49ft)
SOIL Moist but well-drained
HARDINESS Zones 4–8

SUN ☼
PRUNING TIME Winter
SHAPE 🌲

The shagbark hickory is a large, vigorous, deciduous tree with a broadly conical shape. Its ornamental bark, in shades of gray and brown, is a feature all year round, although it does not begin to flake off in the large pieces suggested by its name until it is around 20 years old. The leaves are large, made up of five elongated, ovate leaflets with delicate pointed tips and slightly serrated edges. The foliage is dark green in spring and summer and then puts on an excellent display of pure golden yellow in the fall. Long, yellowish-green male catkins and shorter female catkins are produced on the same tree in spring. If the weather conditions suit it, the pollinated flowers of the female catkins mature into edible nuts held in hard shells, green at first, each up to 2½in (6cm) long.

TREE CARE For the best production of nuts and fall color, plant in a sheltered spot in full sun, with a south- or west-facing aspect. This tree does not like clay or compacted soils that would impede the growth of its deep tap root. Newly planted trees will need regular watering while their roots establish. Prune in winter while the tree is dormant, but only if necessary to remove damaged, dead, or diseased branches or any that are badly placed within the crown on a younger tree.

The golden-yellow leaves of the shagbark hickory tree light up a yard during the fall.

In autumn, the Japanese cornelian cherry puts on a display of colorful leaves and berries.

JAPANESE CORNELIAN CHERRY *CORNUS OFFICINALIS*

HEIGHT & SPREAD up to 26 × 26ft (8 × 8m)
SOIL Well-drained/moist but well-drained
HARDINESS Zones 5–8

SUN ☼ ☼
PRUNING TIME Winter
SHAPE 🌳

The Japanese cornelian cherry forms an upright small tree with an oval crown at first but becomes more spreading with age. It can also be grown as a multi-stemmed specimen. It is deciduous, with much seasonal interest. The leaves are ovate with a pointed tip and a slight upward fold along the central midrib, which becomes more exaggerated in the fall. They are mid- or dark green in spring and summer, turning red, orange, and purple in autumn. The delicate flowers are produced in late winter and early spring, before the leaves emerge: the bright yellow blooms are held in tiny clusters 1in (2.5cm) across. Elongated, oblong, and edible fruits that swell through the summer ripen in the fall to scarlet. Older trees have more ruffled, peeling dark brown bark.

TREE CARE This tree performs best in a fertile, rich, moist but well-drained, and neutral to acidic soil (see *pp.26–27*). It will tolerate some shade and exposure, preferring a cool spot in summer, but do not plant it in north-facing aspects. Water newly planted trees while they establish. Some formative pruning to create a balanced framework of branches can be helpful, but once mature, the only pruning necessary is to remove any damaged, dead, or diseased branches in winter when the tree is dormant.

The fall flowers of the seven son flower tree provide useful late-season nectar and pollen for insects.

SEVEN SON FLOWER TREE *HEPTACODIUM MICONIOIDES*

HEIGHT & SPREAD 20 × 10ft (6 × 3m)
SOIL Well-drained/moist but well-drained
HARDINESS Zones 5–9

SUN ☼ ☀
PRUNING TIME Winter
SHAPE 🌳

This bushy, upright small tree is also known as *Hepaticum jasminoides* and the seven son flower of Zhejiang. Its deciduous foliage emerges a bright lime green in spring, turns dark green in summer, and takes on purple tinges in the fall. The leaves are an elongated oval shape with a pointed tip, up to 6in (15cm) long, with wavy margins giving them a slightly crinkled effect; three prominent veins run parallel from the leaf stalk to the tip. However, the flowers rather than the foliage provide its fall color. Profuse clusters of fragrant, white, star-shaped blooms with narrow petals are produced while the tree still has its leaves. After flowering, the pale green petal-like leaves (the calyx) at the base of the flower turn bright shades of pink, purple, and red. On older wood, the bark peels attractively in long strips.

TREE CARE Plant in a sheltered position, avoiding a north-facing aspect if possible, in full sun or light dappled shade. It will grow well in any soil type other than wet. Young trees will need regular watering while their roots establish. This tree should not need pruning, but if the removal of damaged, dead, or diseased branches is needed, carry this out in winter while the tree is dormant. Take out any badly placed or congested branches at the same time if required.

SWEET GUM *LIQUIDAMBAR STYRACIFLUA*

HEIGHT & SPREAD Up to 65 × 26ft (20 × 8m)
SOIL Well-drained/moist but well-drained
HARDINESS Zones 5–9

SUN ☼ ☀
PRUNING TIME Winter
SHAPE 🌲

The glossy deciduous leaves of the sweet gum are bright to mid-green in spring and summer, turning in the fall to dark tints of plum as well as brighter oranges, golds, scarlet, and crimson; the brightest colors start at the apex and move down the tree as the season progresses. The leaves are five- or seven-lobed with narrow points, similar to maples, and almost star-shaped. It is a moderately slow-growing tree with a broadly conical outline and a corky bark displaying characteristic fissures. Good varieties of sweet gum include 'Worplesdon' and 'Penwood'; the latter retains its leaves longer than other varieties and the species in autumn.

TREE CARE Grow the sweet gum tree in soil with an acidic or neutral pH (see pp.26–27) and a sheltered or exposed position. It will grow well in full sun or partial shade, but be sure to give it a prominent position where you can best admire its spectacular rainbow of colors. Water a newly planted tree regularly for two years while the roots establish. To create a balanced framework of branches for the crown, young trees can be given some formative pruning in winter while the tree is dormant. Mature trees should need little or no pruning: damaged, dead, or diseased branches can be removed as necessary in winter.

The colorful fall leaves of the sweet gum exude a mango fragrance when crushed.

CRAB APPLE 'BUTTERBALL' *MALUS 'BUTTERBALL'*

HEIGHT & SPREAD 13 × 13ft (4 × 4m)
SOIL Well-drained/moist but well-drained
HARDINESS Zones 3–8
SUN ☀
PRUNING TIME Winter
SHAPE 🌳

The color and shape of the apples on 'Butterball' explain the choice of this variety's name.

'Butterball' is a delightful small crab apple tree with a spreading crown of branches that droop slightly toward the ends. In spring, the leaves emerge light green, maturing to dark green for summer with a paler underside. The blossoms open when the branches are still bare or just as the leaves emerge: the nectar-rich single flowers are held in clusters, pink in bud and opening white with a pink blush, and are popular with pollinating insects. The fall fruits are around 1in (2.5cm) long and a pure buttery-yellow color; they grow in profuse clusters along the length of the branches. Persisting well into winter after the leaves fall, when they can become flushed with orange or red, they are food for wildlife, especially birds. The autumn foliage is also yellow.

TREE CARE Crab apples will flower best, and therefore fruit best, in a sunny spot, preferably sheltered from strong winds and frosts that can damage the blossoms. However, they are tolerant of a wide range of soil types. Some formative pruning will help establish a good framework of branches on the young tree, after which little pruning is needed. Remove dead, diseased, damaged, or badly placed branches in winter. Water young trees regularly while the roots are establishing.

TULEPO *NYSSA SYLVATICA*

HEIGHT & SPREAD Up to 66 × 33ft (20 × 10m)
SOIL Moist but well-drained
HARDINESS Zones 3–9
SUN ☀ ☀
PRUNING TIME Winter
SHAPE 🌲

The tulepo tree is an elegant deciduous tree, slow in growth, forming a broadly conical shape with relatively airy branches. The leaves are ovate with a pointed tip, up to 6in (15cm) in length. In spring and summer they are a glossy mid-green, with a slightly thick, leathery appearance; in the fall they turn bright shades of red, orange, and yellow, each leaf patterned with color as the green recedes toward the central vein. The greenish-white spring flowers, useful for pollinating insects, are followed by inedible, spherical to ovoid, black, berrylike autumn fruits that are popular with birds. The bark is gray, flaky when young, becoming more fissured with age.

TREE CARE This tree prefers a sheltered spot, away from cold winds and deep shade. The fall color depends to an extent on the soil conditions: a rich soil that has an acidic or neutral pH (*see pp.26–27*) is best. Conditions that are moist but well-drained are ideal, and the tulepo can tolerate brief periods of waterlogging around its roots—it's a good choice for a spot near a stream or river. Water young plants regularly for at least two years after planting, until their roots are established. This tree should not require pruning, but any dead, damaged, or diseased branches can be removed in winter while it is dormant.

Plant tulepo trees where their autumn color can be appreciated in all its detail.

PERSIAN IRONWOOD *PARROTIA PERSICA*

HEIGHT & SPREAD Up to 26 × 33ft (8 × 10m)
SOIL Well-drained/moist but well-drained
HARDINESS Zones 5–8
SUN ☼ ☼
PRUNING TIME Winter
SHAPE 🌳

Persian ironwood is a wide-spreading, deciduous tree with a low crown of silvery-gray, gnarled branches that give it architectural interest even in winter. It can be grown on a short trunk or as a multi-stemmed tree. The leaves are ovate, leathery, and deeply ribbed with veins. Emerging a bright lime green, they mature to dark green in summer before the color starts to recede into the veins in the fall, revealing glorious tints of plum and crimson, highlighted with scarlet, orange, and yellow. The leaves change color gradually and are held on the branches for many weeks, extending the display through the season. The flowers bloom on bare branches in late winter or early spring; they are prolific but tiny and without petals, each one just a cluster of dark red stamens.

TREE CARE Plant Persian ironwood in any soil other than wet and in full sun or partial shade. It tolerates windy sites and requires little maintenance. Water young trees regularly while their roots establish. Mature trees do not require regular pruning, and this species' dense, solid wood makes them hard to cut. Remove dead, damaged, or diseased branches in early to midwinter while the tree is dormant. Misplaced branches can be left to enhance the wrought, tangled appearance of the crown.

The leaves of the Persian ironwood display all their fall colors over time, creating a multihued appearance.

The vivid fall colors of the stag's horn sumac light up the garden like a beacon.

STAG'S HORN SUMAC *RHUS TYPHINA*

HEIGHT & SPREAD Up to 20 × 13ft (6 × 4m)
SOIL Moist but well-drained
HARDINESS Zones 4–8
SUN ☼
PRUNING TIME Winter
SHAPE 🌳

This sumac is a small, deciduous tree or large shrub with an airy crown. Grown on a short trunk or as a multi-stemmed specimen, it readily produces suckers that can be removed or a few allowed to remain to create a little grove. The leaves are divided into long, thin leaflets with serrated edges, which hang down from either side of the stalk, becoming more pendulous into the fall. The foliage is mid- to dark green in spring and summer, but in the fall displays reds, oranges, and yellows. Female trees produce large, dense, cone-shaped seedpods that are held upright on the branches in the fall, persisting into winter and keeping their pinkish-red color throughout. The wood is covered with a down of short red-brown hairs, softer on younger branches, like a stag's antlers.

TREE CARE Wear gloves when handling this tree, as it can cause severe skin irritation. It will grow in most sunny positions and soil types other than wet; avoid a north-facing aspect. Water young trees regularly. Stag's horn sumac does not need pruning but can be cut back to improve the shape or reduce its size. To remove suckers, tear them out as deep in the soil as possible, which removes more buds than cutting. For trees planted in lawns, keep the suckers under control by regular mowing.

JAPANESE ROWAN *SORBUS COMMIXTA*

HEIGHT & SPREAD 20 × 13ft (6 × 4m)
SOIL Well-drained/moist but well-drained
HARDINESS Zones 5–9

SUN ☼ ☼
PRUNING TIME Winter
SHAPE 🌲

The Japanese rowan is a good choice of a compact, deciduous tree for autumn color: it has a neat habit with relatively upright branches, giving it a broadly conical outline. The foliage is mid-green in spring and summer, but turns vivid reds and oranges in the fall. The leaves are made up of several small, opposite pairs of leaflets, each elongated with a pointed tip and a slightly toothed edge. In spring, the tree is covered with 6in (15cm) wide flat-topped heads of small, creamy-white flowers. These are followed by drooping clusters of berries that ripen to scarlet, adding to the brilliance of the fall display. The berries are edible once cooked and can be used to make preserves, such as rowan jelly; they are a very popular food for birds as well.

TREE CARE Plant Japanese rowan trees in a neutral or acidic soil (see pp.26–27), as they will not do well in chalky or limy conditions. They tolerate windy, exposed sites and can be grown in full sun or partial shade. Water newly planted trees regularly while their roots establish. Formative pruning will help create a balanced framework of branches, but it is not essential. Mature trees will need only any damaged, dead, or diseased branches taken out. Carry out pruning in winter, while the tree is dormant.

The foliage of the Japanese rowan takes on fiery tones of brilliant red and orange during the fall.

The pink berries of 'Pink Pagoda' persist on the tree all through the fall, paling in color as the season progresses.

HUPEH ROWAN *SORBUS PSEUDOHUPEHENSIS* 'PINK PAGODA'

HEIGHT & SPREAD 20 × 10ft (6 × 3m)
SOIL Well-drained/moist but well-drained
HARDINESS Zones 3–8

SUN ☼ ☼
PRUNING TIME Winter
SHAPE 🌳

'Pink Pagoda' is a neat tree with a bushy, deciduous crown and attractively gray-patterned bark on its smooth trunk. The leaves are composed of opposite pairs of smaller leaflets, which are ovate with rounded tips. In spring and summer, the foliage is a glaucous color that complements the white blossoms and pink berries that follow. The flowers are small but held in large, flat, fluffy-looking clusters in late spring and early summer. Over the summer, they develop into substantial bunches of berries; starting a rosy-pink color, they ripen to paler pink or white in the fall, adding to the display from the foliage, which by then has turned shades of red, purple, and orange. The berries are held on the tree into winter, providing late-season food for wildlife, or they can be harvested for cooking—they are toxic when raw.

TREE CARE Hupeh rowan trees will grow well in sun or partial shade and tolerate exposure to wind. They like a neutral or acidic soil (see pp.26–27) and will need regular watering after planting while their roots establish. Prune only to remove any damaged, dead, or diseased branches in winter. Young trees can be given some optional formative pruning to create a balanced framework of branches in the crown.

MAPLE *ACER* SPECIES

The maple family includes many trees that produce colorful stems in winter. Choose from the paperbark maple, with its dramatic peeling bark, or one of the snake-bark maples, which sport striped stems in a range of colors. Growing into small to medium-size trees, they are ideal for an urban garden and need little aftercare or pruning once established. Most offer a blaze of fiery foliage in the fall, too.

HEIGHT & SPREAD up to 39 × 26ft (12 × 8m)
SOIL Moist but well-drained
HARDINESS Zones 5–9
SUN ☼ ☼
PRUNING TIME Autumn/winter
SHAPE 🌳

Peeling, coppery-colored bark adorns the paperbark maple (*Acer griseum*).

The snake-bark maple (*Acer capillipes*) has dramatic white-striped stems.

ALSO TRY

The following maples also provide dramatic bark interest in winter:

- **Père David's maple** (*Acer davidii*) The young red shoots of this spreading tree evolve to produce green and white stripes as they mature. It grows a little larger than other acers and so is a good choice for a medium-sized yard.
- **Coral bark maple** (*Acer palmatum* 'Sango-kaku') The young bright coral-red shoots of this small tree can persist through winter, while more emerge in early spring, creating a dazzling display.

CHOOSING A MAPLE

The best maples for winter bark interest include the paperbark maple (*Acer griseum*), and the snake-bark maples *Acer capillipes* and *Acer rufinerve*. The paperbark features dramatic cinnamon-colored peeling bark that looks spectacular when the tree is planted in a spot where the low winter light catches the stems. *A. capillipes* sports decorative gray and white striped bark, while that of *A. rufinerve* is green and white. These maples also feature green lobed leaves that glow in the fall when the foliage fires up, taking on shades of bright orange and red. They are slow-growing and ideal for small gardens, taking more than 20 years to reach their final mature height and spread. Multi-stemmed trees will provide the maximum impact.

TREE CARE Maples like a sunny or partly shaded position in any free-draining soil—a little acidity is ideal, but they will still thrive in neutral or slightly alkaline conditions. Keep plants well watered during dry spells for the first two years until the roots are established. These trees require little pruning—simply remove dead, diseased, and crossing stems after leaf fall to prevent sap bleeding from the stems.

LIFTING THE CANOPY

You can make the most of these maples' colorful stems at other times of the year by lifting the canopy to show off more of the trunk. To do this, remove the lower branches when the tree is dormant in late fall or winter to expose more of the bark when the leaves unfurl in spring.

WEST HIMALAYAN BIRCH *BETULA UTILIS* SUBSP. *JACQUEMONTII*

HEIGHT & SPREAD 39 × 26ft (12 × 8m)
SOIL Moist but well-drained
HARDINESS Zones 5–8

SUN ☼ ☼
PRUNING TIME Autumn/early winter
SHAPE 🌲

Birches are prized for their decorative white stems that gleam in the pale winter sun, creating ghostly silhouettes in the garden throughout the colder months. The best in this respect is the West Himalayan birch. A good choice for a medium-sized garden, this beautiful tree appeals on many levels. It sports dark green oval leaves that turn buttery yellow in autumn before falling, and its yellow-brown catkins dance on the bare stems in early spring. In smaller gardens, try *Betula utilis* 'Snow Queen', which is a more compact form. Another option for the medium-sized yard is the Erman's birch (*Betula ermanii*), which produces creamy-white bark that peels away to reveal a pinkish-brown layer, creating a two-tone effect.

Most birches grow quickly into statuesque trees, so ensure you have space to allow yours to develop. Multi-stemmed trees won't grow quite as large as those with single trunks.

TREE CARE Plant in any reasonably well-drained soil. Water well during dry spells until the roots are established. These trees require little pruning, apart from the removal of dead, diseased, damaged, or crossing stems in late fall. Also rub out any shoots on the lower trunk to keep it clear.

Gleaming white stems that create drama in the depths of winter make the West Himalayan birch a top choice.

The peeling mahogany-colored stems of the Tibetan cherry will glow in weak winter sunlight.

TIBETAN CHERRY *PRUNUS SERRULA*

HEIGHT & SPREAD up to 33 × 20ft (10 × 6m)
SOIL Moist but well-drained
HARDINESS Zones 6–8

SUN ☼
PRUNING TIME Late winter/early spring
SHAPE 🌳

The Tibetan cherry is grown primarily for its gleaming mahogany-colored bark rather than the small white spring flowers and inedible fruits that follow. However, while they are not particularly eye-catching, the blooms will attract bees and other pollinators. The colorful stems are decorated with horizontal cream bands, and the bark also peels to reveal a fresh bronze-red layer beneath. Try to find a spot for this tree where the sun will illuminate the stems during the winter months. The slim green leaves turn a rich shade of yellow before falling in autumn. A good choice for a medium-sized garden, the Tibetan cherry can reach up to 33ft (10m) in height; for a smaller space, choose a multi-stemmed specimen, which will remain more compact and produce a dramatic display of the beautiful stems.

TREE CARE This cherry is not too fussy about the soil, growing well in most types, except heavy clays prone to waterlogging. After planting, keep it well watered during dry spells for the first two or three years until the roots are established. It also benefits from formative pruning to create a balanced shape (see p.129), after which you will simply need to remove dead, diseased, and crossing stems, cutting it in summer.

KATSURA TREE *CERCIDIPHYLLUM JAPONICUM*

HEIGHT & SPREAD up to 33 × 26ft (10 × 8m)
SOIL Well-drained/moist but well-drained
HARDINESS Zones 4–8

SUN ☼ ☼
PRUNING TIME Winter
SHAPE 🌢 🌳

The katsura is an elegant, medium-sized tree with a compact crown of numerous small branches, giving a lacy appearance. Conical in shape when young, it then matures into a more spreading, rounded tree. The heart-shaped deciduous leaves are around 4in (10cm) long, with many distinct veins that give the leaf surface a slightly bumpy appearance. They unfurl a coppery or bronzed purple color in spring, turning lime green in summer. In the fall, they take on all the colors of the season—red, orange, yellow, purple, and pink—and also develop a strong, delicious smell reminiscent of caramel. They remain fragrant after falling; walking over the fallen leaves revives the aroma. Katsura trees are either male or female—they have slightly different flowers, but both types are small, and the fruits are insignificant.

TREE CARE Plant in a sheltered spot in full sun or dappled shade where it will be protected from late frosts; choose a site where you will be able to appreciate the fragrance. Katsura trees prefer neutral or acidic soils (the best fall color will be in an acidic soil; see pp.26–27); water trees regularly after planting while their roots establish in the soil. Prune in winter, but only if it is necessary to remove any dead, damaged, or diseased branches.

The fragrant fall leaves of the katsura tree emit the toffee-apple scents of the season.

HANDKERCHIEF TREE *DAVIDIA INVOLUCRATA*

HEIGHT & SPREAD Up to 49 × 33ft (15 × 10m)
SOIL Well-drained/moist but well-drained
HARDINESS Zones 6–8

SUN ☼ ☼
PRUNING TIME Winter
SHAPE 🌲

The eponymous "handkerchief" of this tree helps attract insects to pollinate its flowers.

The handkerchief tree, also known as the ghost or dove tree, is a medium to large deciduous specimen that forms a broadly conical shape. Its leaves are bright green and up to 6in (15cm) long, broadly ovate with a sharply serrated edge and pointed tip, and softly hairy on the underside. They give off a spicy fragrance when they emerge in spring. In summer, small, spherical flowers are produced, surrounded by a pair of unequal, large, white, pendulous bracts (petal-like leaves). It can take 10 years or more for trees to start flowering, but once they are mature, the flowers and bracts are produced in profusion. The tree has no remarkable color in the fall, but nutlike seeds the size of golf balls hang singly on long stalks and are often held on the tree well into winter; the peeling cinnamon-brown bark offers added winter interest.

TREE CARE The handkerchief tree will grow well in most soils and sun or partial shade, but it requires a sheltered spot out of cold winds and a relatively warm average climate to thrive. Water young trees regularly while their roots establish. They are low-maintenance and will require only the removal of any damaged, dead, or diseased branches. Carry this out in winter, while the trees are dormant.

VOSS'S LABURNUM *LABURNUM × WATERERI* 'VOSSII'

HEIGHT & SPREAD 16 × 13ft (5 × 4m)
SOIL Well-drained
HARDINESS Zones 5–7

SUN ☼
PRUNING TIME Winter
SHAPE 🌳

Voss's laburnum is a deciduous tree that forms a rounded, spreading crown on a slender trunk. It is an excellent specimen to plant in isolation, so as to best admire its dense cascades of golden-yellow flowers in spring. Each "chain" of flowers can be up to 24in (60cm) long, lasting two to three weeks; they are highly fragrant and popular with pollinators such as bees. Beanlike seedpods follow the flowers, initially green, then in autumn drying to brown before they fall; this tree does not produce as many seedpods as other laburnum varieties. The leaves are glossy and a deep-green color that sets off the golden flowers beautifully; they are made up of three ovate or elliptic leaflets with smooth edges. Note that all parts of the tree and especially the seeds are toxic for both people and animals if eaten.

TREE CARE Plant Voss's laburnum in any well-drained soil. It will tolerate coastal conditions and some exposure to wind, doing best in a bright, sunny position. Water young trees for two years while their roots are establishing. Laburnum trees do not need much pruning—just take off damaged, dead, or diseased branches in winter. Removing the seedpods helps conserve the tree's energy and promotes good flowering the following year but is not essential.

Voss's laburnum is also known as the golden chain tree because of its dangling yellow flowers.

The feathery, aromatic foliage of 'Flamingo' fades from pink to yellow as summer progresses.

CHINESE CEDAR 'FLAMINGO' *TOONA SINENSIS* 'FLAMINGO'

HEIGHT & SPREAD Up to 49 × 33ft (15 × 10m)
SOIL Well-drained
HARDINESS Zones 5–10

SUN ☼
PRUNING TIME Winter
SHAPE 🌲

All parts of this striking tree—the bark, foliage, and flowers—are aromatic. 'Flamingo' forms an upright and broadly columnar tree, with a narrow crown that spreads with age; it can also be grown as a multi-stemmed specimen. The deciduous foliage emerges a vivid salmon pink in spring, fades to creamy yellow and then becomes emerald green in summer, finally turning yellow in the fall. The thin, papery leaves are up to 24in (60cm) long, made up of elongated ovate leaflets in opposite pairs on bright red leaf stalks. In summer, the tree produces dense pendulous clusters up to 12in (30cm) long of fragrant white flowers that are very attractive to insects; these are followed by bunches of winged capsulelike fruits. The bark peels off in long, papery strips as it matures.

TREE CARE 'Flamingo' is only hardy to between 23° and 14°F (–5° and –10°C), so it needs a sheltered spot in full sun and a warm climate. Ensure that the soil is well-drained so the tree will not be sitting in soggy soil over winter and is not exposed to strong or cold winds; avoid planting in a north-facing aspect. Water newly planted trees regularly. Mature trees should need little maintenance. If any branches are damaged, dead, or diseased, these can be pruned out in winter.

The vine maple, like many *Acer* species, has spectacular fall color that lights up the yard on sunny days.

VINE MAPLE *ACER CIRCINATUM*

HEIGHT & SPREAD 26 × 20ft (8 × 6m)
SOIL Moist but well-drained
HARDINESS Zones 6–9

SUN ☼ ☼
PRUNING TIME Winter
SHAPE 🌳

The vine maple is a small, bushy tree on a shortish trunk that can also be grown as a large, multi-stemmed, spreading shrub. It is deciduous and holds its foliage in a tiered canopy. The leaves emerge acid green in spring, darkening to mid-green in summer; in fall, they turn vivid reds, oranges, and yellows. The points on the seven to nine lobes are short, giving the leaves an overall rounded shape. Clusters of small purple and white flowers with only moderate levels of pollen appear in spring, followed by the typical winged seedpods, starting red and ripening to brown as they dry in fall. These seeds are a useful food source for birds and small mammals.

TREE CARE Plant the vine maple in any aspect except north-facing; it handles exposure to wind and cold and most soils except chalk. Water newly planted trees regularly while their roots establish in the soil. It is not necessary to prune the vine maple, but it does benefit from some formative and maintenance pruning to keep it an attractive shape with a balanced and healthy framework of branches in the crown. In late fall to midwinter, remove any damaged, dead, or diseased limbs, plus any duplicated branches (two growing the same way, but one above the other) and those that are crossing or otherwise badly placed.

HOLLY 'HANDSWORTH NEW SILVER' *ILEX* 'HANDSWORTH NEW SILVER'

HEIGHT & SPREAD 13 × 8ft (4 × 2.5m)
SOIL Well-drained/moist but well-drained
HARDINESS Zones 7–9

SUN ☼ ☼
PRUNING TIME Summer
SHAPE 🌳

Hollies are dioecious, which means that they produce male and female flowers on different plants. Females such as 'Handsworth New Silver' are a good choice if you suffer from allergies: they don't produce pollen. This holly is a slow-growing evergreen that forms a bushy, rounded small tree; it has a dense, compact crown that can be left to grow naturally or clipped into a neater shape. Its long, narrow leaves have an irregular, dark green oval in the center and creamy-white margins to the edges. The new shoots are tinged with purple. In late spring and early summer, the tree produces small white flowers, which, if pollinated, are followed by the berries,

bright green at first and ripening to red. These are a popular winter food for birds but toxic if ingested by people or pets.

TREE CARE Grown in partial or dappled shade, this tree will produce fewer flowers (and therefore berries) than if grown in full sun. It is tolerant of all soils, other than wet, and will grow well in coastal situations and those exposed to wind. Water young trees regularly until their roots establish. Prune in mid- to late summer to remove any damaged, dead, or diseased branches. To shape a tree, lightly trim the foliage with hedging shears or remove whole or parts of branches to sculpt the crown.

The leaves of 'Handsworth New Silver' have an irregular white margin, giving a tricolored effect with the red berries.

Light green young leaves and white flowers give the northern Japanese magnolia a fresh spring look.

NORTHERN JAPANESE MAGNOLIA *MAGNOLIA KOBUS*

HEIGHT & SPREAD Up to 33 × 16ft (10 × 5m)
SOIL Well-drained/moist but well-drained
HARDINESS Zones 5–8

SUN ☼☀
PRUNING TIME Summer to early fall
SHAPE 🌲

This deciduous tree has a relatively slender, upright form compared with other magnolias, although it still has a broadly conical habit. The fragrant, goblet-shaped flowers are about 4in (10cm) wide and open in early or mid-spring; they contain heavy pollen that is transferred by insects rather than by wind and poses less of a problem for allergy sufferers. The trees do not start flowering until they are 12–15 years old, but once mature will put on a profuse display each year. The pink, candlelike fruits that follow split open in autumn to reveal scarlet seeds. The leaves are obovate and up to 6in (15cm) long, with smooth edges. They emerge acid green in spring, mature to mid-green for summer, and yellow slightly before they fall with the first frosts in autumn.

TREE CARE Magnolias are hardy trees, but to thrive they need shelter from harsh winds and the worst of the winter cold, which could cause the spring flowers to brown and fall prematurely. This species prefers a neutral or acidic soil but, unlike many other magnolias, will tolerate more alkaline conditions (see pp.26–27). Water young trees regularly, especially in dry spells. Remove any dead, diseased, or damaged wood, if necessary, pruning between midsummer and early fall.

APPLE AND CRAB APPLE SPECIES *MALUS* SPECIES

HEIGHT & SPREAD Up to 13 × 13ft (4 × 4m)
SOIL Moist but well-drained
HARDINESS Zones 2–8

SUN ☼
PRUNING TIME Winter and summer
SHAPE 🌳🌳🌲🌲🌲

All apple and crab apple species and varieties are a suitable choice for an allergy-friendly garden because their flowers are not wind-pollinated. There are many varieties available (see *Malus domestica*, p.83), and when grown on appropriate rootstocks, they can be small and compact or larger and spreading. Crab apples also produce edible fruit, but the apples are much smaller and can be very bitter: to make them palatable, they can be cooked with sugar to make preserves, such as crab apple jelly. However, they are very ornamental on the bare branches and make useful food for birds and other wildlife in the winter.

TREE CARE Crab apple and apple trees fruit best in a sunny position, sheltered from frost and cold winds that can damage the blossom. Water young trees and those grown in containers regularly; mature trees may also need watering during very dry spells, especially when they are flowering and fruiting. Prune apple trees to establish a strong framework in the first few years, then continue to prune every winter to maintain them, taking out dead and diseased branches, removing crossing branches, and shortening new growth. Crab apple trees need only damaged, dead, or diseased branches to be removed as necessary.

Apple and crab apple blossoms, here on crab 'Golden Hornet', are usually white or pink.

PLUM *PRUNUS DOMESTICA*

HEIGHT & SPREAD Up to 13 × 13ft (4 × 4m)
SOIL Well-drained/moist but well-drained
HARDINESS Zones 5–7

SUN ☼
PRUNING TIME Summer
SHAPE 🌳🟦▮

The *Prunus* family, which includes ornamental and fruiting cherries as well as *P. domestica*, the fruiting plum, all produce blossoms in spring that have a low impact on allergy sufferers because their sticky pollen is retained in the flowers, which are pollinated by insects rather than being dispersed by wind. There are many varieties available and different ways to grow them; see also p.82 for more information on growing plum 'Victoria'. The leaves are deciduous, ovate, and dark green, turning yellow, orange, or red in the fall, depending on the variety. The white single flowers appear as the leaves unfurl, or shortly afterward.

TREE CARE Plant plum trees in a sunny, warm, sheltered location, or train them against a sunny wall, which will help the fruit ripen. They grow well in most soils but do not like wet or waterlogged conditions. Water newly planted trees regularly as their roots establish; mature edible fruit trees may need watering in prolonged dry spells, especially when flowering and fruiting. Prune in midsummer or after harvesting the fruit to maintain the crown of a freestanding tree in an open-centered goblet shape; take out dead, damaged, or diseased wood and any branches that are crossing the center of the crown or crowding other, better-placed stems.

Plum trees deliver generous amounts of edible fruit in summer, while also being suitable for those with a pollen allergy.

ALMOND *PRUNUS DULCIS*

HEIGHT & SPREAD Up to 13 × 13ft (4 × 4m)
SOIL Moist but well-drained
HARDINESS Zones 7–9

SUN ☼
PRUNING TIME Summer
SHAPE 🌳🟦▮

The almond tree blooms very early in spring, when the colder, wetter weather can keep the pollen count low, but this also means that harvests may be reduced if the blossoms are damaged by the weather or if pollination, which is performed by insects, is reduced. The tree has an elegant, upright form with a spreading crown, or it can be trained as a fan against a wall. The sweetly scented blossoms emerge before the leaves; the single, cup-shaped flowers have white or pink petals, depending on the variety. The leaves are lance-shaped with toothed edges, mid-green in summer, then turning yellow in the fall. Almond nuts will be ready to harvest in the fall.

TREE CARE Although the trees are hardy, the flowers are susceptible to damage from frost, cold winds, and wet weather. To enjoy the blossoms and maybe get some almonds to pick, plant in a very sunny, warm, sheltered location or train the tree against a sunny wall. Young trees will need regular watering as their roots establish; water mature trees during prolonged dry spells, especially when flowering and fruiting. Prune in midsummer or after the harvest. For a freestanding tree, take out any dead, damaged, or diseased wood, plus any crossing, crowded, or otherwise misplaced branches to keep the crown in an open-centered goblet shape.

Almond blossoms are produced in abundance on the tree's leafless branches in early spring.

CALLERY PEAR 'CHANTICLEER' *PYRUS CALLYREANA* 'CHANTICLEER'

HEIGHT & SPREAD 16 × 10ft (5 × 3m)
SOIL Well-drained/moist but well-drained
HARDINESS Zones 4–8

SUN ☀
PRUNING TIME Winter
SHAPE ▮

Their dense crowns make 'Chanticleer' pear trees ideal to use as a tall screen above a wall or fence.

The pear family (*Pyrus* species), including both edible pears (*P. communis*) and ornamental forms such as 'Chanticleer', are all suitable for a low-allergy garden because their pollen is not dispersed by wind; the blooms are insect-pollinated. 'Chanticleer' forms an elegant, slender, medium-sized tree with a narrowly conical dense crown that makes it ideal for small yards or for creating an avenue, adding structure and height without casting too much shade. Very tolerant of urban air pollution, it has glossy dark-green deciduous foliage that makes a good backdrop for the white blossoms in spring, which are held in small, dangling clusters. In the fall, the leaves turn rich, vivid reds and buttery yellows, holding well on the tree, and the small fruits ripen to greenish-brown. They are edible, but generally very bitter.

TREE CARE 'Chanticleer' will grow well in a sunny garden and tolerates some exposure to wind and cold. This tree thrives in fertile, moist but well-drained soil but, once well-established, will tolerate periods of drought, its deep roots tapping into moisture at lower levels in the ground. However, water newly planted trees regularly until their roots are established. Prune in winter, if necessary, to remove dead, damaged, or diseased branches.

ROWAN *SORBUS AUCUPARIA*

HEIGHT & SPREAD Up to 49 × 23ft (15 × 7m)
SOIL Well-drained/moist but well-drained
HARDINESS Zones 3–6

SUN ☀ ☀
PRUNING TIME Winter
SHAPE 🌳

Rowan trees are especially good for wildlife, their profusion of berries supplying food for birds in the fall.

Also known as the mountain ash, the rowan tree is a very hardy, upright, deciduous tree with a spreading crown. It grows quickly when young, and the trunk tends to split into several thick, erect branches, giving it a multi-stemmed appearance. The smooth, slightly shiny bark is attractively mottled in shades of silvery gray and white, while the leaves are made up of several opposite pairs of small leaflets on a reddish stalk, narrowly ovate with toothed edges. They are mid-green in spring and summer, turning yellow in the fall. In spring, the tree produces slightly domed clusters of small white flowers that are insect-pollinated and so produce little or no airborne pollen. They are followed by clusters of berries that ripen to red in late summer; the berries are poisonous when raw but can be eaten once cooked.

TREE CARE Rowan trees can be planted in any soil other than wet and in a sunny or partially shaded site. They also tolerate exposure to wind, cold, air pollution, and coastal spray. Water newly planted trees regularly. Some formative pruning of young trees will help create a balanced framework of branches, but it is not essential. Prune older trees in winter to remove any damaged, dead, diseased, or crossing branches.

ECO-FRIENDLY TREES

Trees that produce blossoms, catkins, fruits, or nuts will provide a feast for pollinating insects, birds, and other garden wildlife, while many offer nesting and roosting sites too. Trees also benefit the environment by capturing and storing carbon dioxide, an airborne pollutant that is partly responsible for climate change. Those listed in the "Trees for maximum carbon capture" section are among the most eco-friendly, according to research conducted in the UK into the pollution filtration and carbon capture and storage capacity of the trees over their lifespan.

FIELD MAPLE *ACER CAMPESTRE*

HEIGHT & SPREAD up to 39 × 13ft (12 × 4m)
SOIL Moist but well-drained
HARDINESS Zones 5–8

SUN ☼ ☼
PRUNING TIME Winter
SHAPE 🌳

The field maple forms a medium-sized deciduous tree, holding its branches in a compact, bushy crown. It is tolerant of air pollution, making it a good choice for gardens near roads and in cities. The leaves are palmate, with five blunted lobes, mid-green in summer, then turning yellow in the fall, sometimes with a red tinge. Aphids suck sap from them, making the tree popular with insects and birds that eat the aphids and their sticky "honeydew" excretions. Moths also use field maples for laying their eggs so that their caterpillars can eat the leaves. The insignificant but abundant green flowers are valuable to insects for their nectar and pollen. They develop into the seeds that are held in clusters and form the winged "helicopters" loved by children. The seeds are green with pink edges, ripening to brown in the fall, when they are popular with birds and small mammals.

TREE CARE Field maples are tolerant of most soils and locations. Water young trees while they are establishing, especially during dry weather. Prune only to remove dead, diseased, or damaged branches and any that are crossing or otherwise disrupting the balance of the crown. Take these out after the leaves have fallen, but no later than midwinter or the rising sap will bleed from the pruning wounds.

The golden leaves of the field maple light up beautifully during sunny fall days.

COMMON ALDER *ALNUS GLUTINOSA*

HEIGHT & SPREAD 39 × 20ft (12 × 6m)
SOIL Moist but well-drained/poorly drained
HARDINESS Zones 3–7

SUN ☼
PRUNING TIME Winter
SHAPE 🌲

The female catkins on alder trees, held in groups of three or more, are a good source of food for birds.

Alder trees are ideal for boggy ground as they will tolerate, and indeed draw strength from, growing in waterlogged soil. The leaf buds are gray-purple, opening into mid-green leaves with crinkled edges. These are food for the caterpillars of various butterflies and moths. Catkins emerge before the leaves, adding interest in late winter and offering nectar and pollen to insects including bumblebees; both male and female catkins are produced on the tree. The males are about 2in (5cm) long, green then turning yellow; the females are more rounded. The latter look like little green cones and, once pollinated, they harden and change to a brown color in the fall, eventually releasing seeds that are a popular food for birds, especially siskins and goldfinches.

TREE CARE Alder trees need soil that is consistently moist and prefer a site in full sun; stake the tree for a year or two if it is in an exposed spot. Water newly planted trees as they establish their roots. Alders do not require regular pruning once mature but can be cut in winter while the tree is dormant to remove any dead, diseased, or damaged branches and any crossing stems, if necessary. Some formative pruning when the tree is young will help establish a balanced framework.

HAZEL *CORYLUS AVELLANA*

HEIGHT & SPREAD up to 26 × 26ft (8 × 8m)
SOIL Moist but well-drained/well-drained
HARDINESS Zones 4–8

SUN ☼ ☼
PRUNING TIME Winter
SHAPE 🌳

The hazel, which is also known as the cobnut or common filbert, grows as a multi-stemmed clump of upright branches that provide shelter for ground-nesting birds, such as the yellowhammer, nightingale, and nightjar. The leaves are rounded with a pointed tip, mid-green with a serrated edge and hairy underside; they turn yellow in the fall. Many species of moth caterpillar feed on the leaves in summer. Catkins are produced on bare branches in late winter: the male catkins are long, yellow, and pendulous, while the females are insignificant. Providing some early pollen for bees and bumblebees, they need pollinating by another hazel tree to produce nuts. These are held in clusters on the branches, enclosed in a leafy husk that is pale green at first, turning brown into the fall as they ripen. They are eaten by many birds and also small mammals, especially the endangered hazel dormouse.

TREE CARE Plant hazel trees in full sun or partial shade; they will also tolerate exposed positions. Water young trees in dry spells. Prune by taking out a selection of the older, larger branches each year back to their base in winter. This will keep the tree to a manageable size and will also provide you with bean poles and pea sticks for the garden.

Hazelnuts are often eaten on the tree by squirrels before they fall to the ground for other small mammals to access.

CRAB APPLE 'JELLY KING' *MALUS 'JELLY KING'*

HEIGHT & SPREAD up to 13 × 13ft (4 × 4m)
SOIL Well-drained/moist but well-drained
HARDINESS Zones 3–8

SUN ☼
PRUNING TIME Winter
SHAPE 🌳

All crab apple trees are beneficial for wildlife, but 'Jelly King' is an excellent choice for any garden. A compact, low-maintenance tree, its branches are covered with flowers in spring as the leaves unfurl. Opening from pink buds, the white, single blooms are fragrant and held in clusters; their nectar and pollen are also popular with bees and many other insects. In the fall the crab apples ripen to an orange-red-pink, and are held on the tree well into winter. The fruits are larger than other crab apples, thus providing more food for the wildlife that likes to eat them. Blackbirds and other bird species will peck at the fruits while they are still on the tree, while those that fall will be taken by small mammals preparing to hibernate.

TREE CARE Crab apples flower and fruit best in a sunny spot, sheltered from winds and frosts that can damage the blossoms and so reduce the number of fruits that develop. Formative pruning will help establish a good framework of branches on a young tree, after which little pruning is needed. Simply remove dead, diseased, damaged or badly placed branches in winter. Water trees regularly for the first two years after planting, especially during dry spells, while the roots are establishing.

Crab apple trees bear their blossoms in mid-spring, providing essential food for many pollinators.

BLACKTHORN *PRUNUS SPINOSA*

HEIGHT & SPREAD up to 13 x 13ft (4 x 4m)
SOIL Moist but well-drained
HARDINESS Zones 4–8

SUN ☼
PRUNING TIME Winter/summer
SHAPE 🌳

The blossom of blackthorn is early to emerge in spring, when there are not many other flowers around, so it offers valuable food for insects such as bees. A small deciduous tree, it can be pruned to form a hedge. It has black-purple branches covered in long thorns, but its forbidding crown is useful to small birds as a nesting site. The leaves are small and narrowly oval, pointed with toothed edges; they are mid-green in summer and have no significant fall color. Moths and butterflies lay their eggs on blackthorn trees, as the leaves are food for their caterpillars (which are food for birds). The small, purple-black, berrylike fruits, known as sloes, are edible but very astringent. They are traditionally used to infuse spirits such as gin. Popular with birds and small mammals, they are often eaten before the first frost.

TREE CARE Plant blackthorn trees in full sun and a sheltered site to protect their early blossoms from damage by frost and cold winds. They require no pruning, although you may like to remove some lower branches to create a clear stem and any dead, damaged, or diseased branches. Prune in winter, or in summer to help prevent silver leaf disease from infecting the tree. Remove any suckers around the base of the tree to avoid creating a dense thicket.

The bare branches of the blackthorn tree are covered in white blossoms in early to mid-spring.

The catkins of the gray willow open from tactile buds covered with gray "fur" that resembles a cat's paw.

GOAT WILLOW *SALIX CINEREA*

HEIGHT & SPREAD up to 30 x 13ft (10 x 4m)
SOIL Moist but well-drained/poorly drained
HARDINESS Zones 2–7

SUN ☼
PRUNING TIME Winter
SHAPE 🌳

Goat willow, also known as common sallow, forms a broad, upright, and many-branched tree, slightly scrubby in appearance, but an attractive option for a damp or boggy area of the garden. Its main season of aesthetic interest is late winter and early spring, when the buds on the bare branches swell and become covered with a downy gray fur (giving rise to its other name of pussy willow). These budding branches can be cut for use in floral arrangements. The buds open in early spring into the male catkins, which are short and bright yellow with pollen when ripe; although the tree is wind-pollinated, the pollen is also a useful food source for bumblebees and other insects. Female catkins appear on separate trees (known as dioecious) and are long and green. The slim gray-green leaves feed the caterpillars of many moth and butterfly species. The presence of the larvae in turn attracts birds that seek out the caterpillars and other insect prey among the branches.

TREE CARE Goat willow trees do best where the soil is consistently moist; in the wild they grow beside rivers and streams. Water young trees regularly while their roots establish. Mature trees need little maintenance, but dead, damaged, or diseased branches can be removed in winter.

SMALL-LEAVED LINDEN *TILIA CORDATA*

HEIGHT & SPREAD 39 × 26ft (12 × 8m)
SOIL Well-drained/moist but well-drained
HARDINESS Zones 3–8

SUN ☼ ☼
PRUNING TIME Winter
SHAPE 🌳

Linden trees bear a profusion of small, round, fragrant flowers and pale green leaflike bracts in early summer.

The small-leaved linden forms an attractive upright tree with a large, spreading crown. New branches are smooth and tinged red while the heart-shaped leaves are a bright mid-green, up to 3½in (9cm) long, turning bright yellow in autumn. They are popular with sap-sucking insects such as aphids and as a caterpillar food plant for moth species, so predators (other insects and birds) also flock to the trees. The fragrant flowers are produced in early summer. Small and white, they hang in clusters, each group accompanied by a pale green, leaflike bract that, once the seeds are ready, acts as a sail to help disperse them on the wind. The fragrant flowers are a magnet for pollinating insects, especially bees, and they can also be used to make herbal infusions. The bark is gray and becomes grooved with age.

TREE CARE Linden trees will appreciate being planted in a sheltered spot and are happy in full sun or partial shade. Water newly planted trees during their first two years, especially in dry spells. After a little formative pruning to establish a balanced framework for the crown, lindens need no annual pruning except to remove any dead, damaged, or diseased branches in winter. Remove any suckers from the base as they appear.

GUELDER ROSE *VIBURNUM OPULUS*

HEIGHT & SPREAD 13 × 8ft (4 × 2.5m)
SOIL Well-drained/moist but well-drained
HARDINESS Zones 3–8

SUN ☼ ☼ ☀
PRUNING TIME Spring
SHAPE 🌳

The scarlet berries of the guelder rose hang in pendulous clusters and attract birds in the fall and winter.

The guelder rose is a large shrub or small tree, multi-stemmed with an upright habit and a dense canopy that is used by birds for shelter and as a nesting site. It is deciduous, with three-lobed, mid-green leaves that turn purple or pinkish-red in the fall; they are lightly hairy on their underside. The small creamy-white flowers bloom from late spring to early summer, held in a flat cluster (an umbel), surrounded by larger-petaled but sterile flowers produced by the plant to help it attract pollinators. The flowers are especially attractive to hover flies and butterflies. In autumn, scarlet berries smother the branches. They have an unpleasant smell when broken open and are not edible for people. However, they are an important source of fall and winter food for birds, especially the waxwings and jays.

TREE CARE The guelder rose will grow more or less anywhere and tolerates shade, sun, and exposure equally well. Water newly planted trees while their roots establish. Carry out formative pruning in the first few years to form a tree on a single stem, if desired. After that, the guelder rose needs little annual maintenance. If necessary, to lightly shape it or to remove damaged, dead, or diseased branches, prune in spring or early summer after flowering.

'Fastigiata' hornbeams have a neat flame shape when young, broadening as they mature.

HORNBEAM 'FASTIGIATA' *CARPINUS BETULUS* 'FASTIGIATA'

HEIGHT & SPREAD 49 × 13ft (15 × 4m)
SOIL Moist but well-drained
HARDINESS Zones 4–8

SUN ☼ ☼
PRUNING TIME Winter
SHAPE ⬮

A narrow form of hornbeam better suited to medium-sized or small yards than the species, 'Fastigiata' will still become a sizable tree and store a lot of carbon. Growing quite quickly, it's almost triangular when young, then becomes more oval and broadens with age. Its shape and density make it an architectural addition to the garden. The bright, glossy, mid-green leaves are ovate, with distinct ribbing and serrated edges; in the fall they turn a honeyed yellow. Long green catkins appear in spring, followed by narrow pendulous clusters of winged seeds, green in the summer and brown in autumn before they fall or are eaten by birds.

TREE CARE Hornbeams are tough trees and will do well in exposed conditions, such as coastal areas. Plant as a single tree or put several together in a line to create a tall screen (see *pp.18–19*). Water newly planted trees regularly for two years while they establish. Mature trees need little attention; dead, damaged, or diseased branches can be pruned out in winter while the tree is dormant if necessary. Hornbeams also respond well to trimming into shape, such as into a tighter cone or flame shape as the tree begins to spread. Trim in late summer using a hedge-trimmer or shears; carry out restoration work in winter.

HACKBERRY *CELTIS OCCIDENTALIS*

HEIGHT & SPREAD up to 66 × 33ft (20 × 10m)
SOIL Well-drained
HARDINESS Zones 2–9

SUN ☼
PRUNING TIME Winter
SHAPE ⬮

Celtis occidentalis is also known as the American false elm. Its fruits ripen in late summer and fall. It is a large tree with ascending branches, conical to pyramidal in shape when it is young but more spreading as it matures. The trunk remains relatively slender even as the crown gets larger; the gray bark develops characterful bumps and warts with age. The leaves are ovate, coming to a slender point, green in summer and turning a brassy golden yellow in the fall. The green flowers appear in spring; they are followed by the fruits, which start orange, then ripen through red to a dark purple. They are edible and also very popular with birds.

TREE CARE The American false elm is native to the southern parts of the US and needs a relatively warm and sheltered spot with well-drained soil when grown in a temperate climate. In warmer areas it prefers a less sunny spot with a moister soil. Water young trees regularly for the first two years after planting, especially during dry spells, while their roots establish. These trees require little ongoing maintenance other than to remove any damaged, diseased, or dead branches, which should be done in winter while they are dormant. Badly placed branches can also be removed at this time to create a more balanced crown.

The small flowers of the American false elm are popular with insects such as bees and butterflies.

Eucalyptus foliage is widely used in cut-flower arrangements for its blue-gray color and strong fragrance.

CIDER GUM *EUCALYPTUS GUNNII*

HEIGHT & SPREAD up to 82 × 49ft (25 × 15m)
SOIL Well-drained/moist but well-drained
HARDINESS Zones 8–10

SUN ☼
PRUNING TIME Winter/early spring
SHAPE ▮

Eucalyptus are among the fastest-growing trees in the world, making them good candidates for carbon capture. The cider gum becomes very big indeed but can be cut back hard to keep it to a more appropriate size for your yard. The intensely fragrant evergreen foliage can be used in cut-flower arrangements or in herbal preparations (or simply hang a bunch of young stems in the shower to release their fragrance). The blue-gray leaves are round when juvenile, while older stems and branches have long, lance-shaped leaves. The bark peels away in long strips, giving the trunk a marbled brown and cream appearance. Small white flowers are borne in summer.

TREE CARE Plant in a sheltered, sunny spot. Cider gum trees are tolerant of dry conditions but will grow best in moist but well-drained soils. Keep young trees well watered for two years after planting until their roots are established. If you want to allow the tree to grow to its full extent, no pruning is required except the removal of any damaged, dead, or diseased branches in winter. To keep the tree to a more easily manageable size or to grow for regular foliage supply, cut back hard to a framework of branches (of any size) in early spring. Never pull the peeling bark off the trunk—allow it to fall away naturally.

ENGLISH WALNUT *JUGLANS REGIA*

HEIGHT & SPREAD up to 39 × 26ft (12 × 8m)
SOIL Well-drained/moist but well-drained
HARDINESS Zones 5–9

SUN ☼ ☼
PRUNING TIME Winter
SHAPE 🌳

The English walnut has a thick, relatively short trunk and broadly spreading branches, covered in attractive, fissured, silvery-gray bark when mature. The deciduous foliage is slightly scented when it first emerges, although you may have to crush the leaves to appreciate it fully. They are composed of five to seven leaflets, each roughly oblong, bright to mid-green with pale green veins and bronzed yellow in the fall. The catkins are produced in spring: male catkins are 2–4in (5–10cm) in length, acid green and drooping, while females are shorter and carried in small clusters. In the fall the walnuts develop, surrounded by a pithy green casing that breaks open to reveal the hard brown shell that houses the kernels. These can be eaten fresh from the tree or dried for storing and eating later. Trees can take up to 15 years to start producing nuts regularly.

TREE CARE Planted in full sun and with plenty of space around it, the English walnut will sprawl and spread, but in a woodland situation it will form a more upright tree. It will grow well in most soils; water regularly after planting while the roots establish in the soil. After some formative pruning, walnuts should need little regular attention, but damaged, dead, or diseased branches can be removed in winter as required.

Pick walnuts in autumn, leaving some on the tree as a source of winter food for squirrels.

ANTARCTIC BEECH *NOTHOFAGUS ANTARCTICA*

HEIGHT & SPREAD 39 × 26ft (12 × 8m)
SOIL Moist but well-drained
HARDINESS Zones 5–8

SUN ☼
PRUNING TIME Winter
SHAPE 🌲

The southern hemisphere version of the beech tree *Fagus sylvatica*, the Antarctic beech has a slightly different habit and foliage. It is broadly conical and often multi-stemmed, with an irregular branch structure that creates a relatively light and airy crown. Quite slow-growing, it ultimately forms a very large tree. The bark is dark brown and glossy when young, fading to a more matte pale brown with striking silver/white horizontal dashes ("lenticels"). The leaves are small, dark green, and glossy, with crinkled edges and folds along the veins that give them a charmingly crumpled appearance; in spring, the foliage is sweetly aromatic, and in the fall it turns shades of yellow, orange, and bronze. Inconspicuous but fragrant white flowers are produced in spring, followed by small, inedible nuts.

TREE CARE Plant in a sunny spot and a rich, moist but well-drained, acidic soil (see pp.26–27); newly planted trees will need regular watering while they establish their roots. This tree prefers moist, well-drained soil and tolerates exposure to wind. It can be given some formative pruning in winter to create a single- rather than multi-stemmed tree, if preferred; mature trees need little pruning save to remove any damaged, dead, or diseased branches.

In the fall, the leaves of the Antarctic beech take on yellow, orange, and bronze hues.

PIN OAK *QUERCUS PALUSTRIS*

HEIGHT & SPREAD 33 × 15ft (10 × 5m)
SOIL Well-drained/moist but well-drained
HARDINESS Zones 4–8

SUN ☼ ☼
PRUNING TIME Winter
SHAPE 🌲

The pin oak puts on a stunning display of fall color, with the glossy leaves turning russet and orange.

Oaks are long-lived and large trees, absorbing a lot of carbon as they grow. The elegant pin oak has its main season of interest in autumn, when its leaves turn fiery shades of red and orange before they fall. They are glossy and up to 6in (15cm) long, deeply lobed with pointed tips, mid-green in the summer. The bark is gray and smooth on younger trees, developing shallow vertical furrows as it matures. Catkins in spring are followed by acorns in the fall, although they are not numerous. The tree forms a roughly pyramidal shape on a clear trunk, growing relatively quickly, with a dense crown that becomes more spreading as the tree ages. The upper branches are more or less vertical; the middle ones grow horizontally, while the lower ones droop down. 'Green Pillar' is a more upright variety with a narrower crown that is more suitable for smaller yards.

TREE CARE The pin oak is a strong tree that can tolerate an exposed site, urban air pollution, and short periods of waterlogging as well as drought. Water newly planted trees regularly while their roots establish. Pin oaks are low-maintenance trees, requiring no regular pruning. Dead, damaged, or diseased branches can be pruned out in winter while the tree is dormant.

AMERICAN LINDEN *TILIA AMERICANA*

HEIGHT & SPREAD Up to 98 × 49ft (30 × 15m)
SOIL Well-drained/moist but well-drained
HARDINESS Zones 3–9

SUN ☼ ☼
PRUNING TIME Winter
SHAPE 🌳

The American linden grows quickly into a large, upright tree with an ovate to spreading crown. The large leaves are ovate to heart-shaped, with a pointed tip; they are glossy, dark green and patterned with pale green veins in spring and summer, while the lighter color on the undersides creates a two-tone effect. The foliage then turns yellowy-green in the fall. Small clusters of tiny, scented, creamy-white flowers with a pale green, elongated, leaf-like bract around 4in (10cm) long are produced in early summer. The bracts persist, turning pale brown to help disperse the small spherical seeds on the wind in the fall. The flowers and leaves support a wide range of insect species and their predators (other insects and birds). The bark is smooth and olive or red-tinged when young, paling to a brown-gray with attractive deep vertical ridges when mature.

TREE CARE This tree tolerates some shade but prefers a sheltered spot; after planting, water regularly for two years until the roots are established. After formative pruning to establish a balanced framework for the crown, no annual pruning is needed except to remove any dead, damaged, or diseased branches as necessary. Remove any suckers from the base as they appear.

The mature trunk of the American linden has attractively patterned bark with deep ridges.

JAPANESE ZELKOVA *ZELKOVA SERRATA*

HEIGHT & SPREAD Up to 98 × 59ft (30 × 18m)
SOIL Well-drained/moist but well-drained
HARDINESS Zones 5–8

SUN ☼ ☼
PRUNING TIME Winter
SHAPE 🌳

The Japanese zelkova is valued for its elegant habit that is reminiscent of the elm tree (*Ulmus*). Its upright trunk forks into several large, erect branches that form a semi-open, loose, spreading crown that is attractively architectural both in full leaf and when bare in winter. Relatively fast-growing when young, it slows as it ages. The deciduous leaves are oval to lance shaped, up to 4in (10cm) long, with distinctive veins and toothed edges. A bright grass green in spring, they mature to dark green in summer, then turn yellow and orange, occasionally with red tones, in the fall. The green flowers and fruits are insignificant. The gray bark is smooth when young, but on older wood peels off, revealing orange patches beneath. 'Green Vase' is smaller than the species, forming, as the name suggests, a vase-shaped crown on a shorter trunk.

TREE CARE Ideally, plant in a deep, fertile, and moist but well-drained soil. It will grow well in some shade but prefers a sheltered spot out of cold winds, which can damage the young foliage in spring. It also tolerates urban air pollution well. Water young trees regularly for two years while their roots establish. Little pruning is needed, but damaged, dead, or diseased branches can be removed in winter.

The towering trunks of the Japanese zelkova have textured shaggy bark that peels away to expose orange areas.

MAINTAINING A TREE

Many established trees will look after themselves for long periods, if planted in the soil and garden conditions that suit them, but young trees with immature root systems will require regular watering to promote strong and healthy growth. Older trees may also need some maintenance from time to time, such as pruning to remove dead or diseased wood or wayward branches that are blocking paths or patios. Also familiarize yourself with common pests and diseases so that you can act quickly to minimize any damage they may cause.

WATERING AND FEEDING TREES

Trees planted in the ground are generally easy to maintain, and few need watering and feeding once established. However, young trees require more attention during their first few years, while those in containers need constant care. Young or potted trees may survive winter without much watering, but keep them irrigated in dry spells from spring to fall. Do not feed a tree in winter when it is dormant.

Young trees such as these cherries will need regular watering during the first two or three years after planting.

Water immediately after planting and then regularly for the first two growing seasons to keep the soil moist but not wet.

WATERING NEWLY PLANTED TREES

The roots of most trees take a couple of years to establish and will need regular irrigation throughout this period, particularly from spring to fall, when the plants are in active growth. As a safety precaution, also water during prolonged periods of dry weather in the third year after planting, in case the roots have not fully developed and still need some extra moisture. After that, if you have planted the right tree in the right place, it should survive on rainfall alone, without any extra irrigation, except during an exceptionally long period of drought.

When watering, use a hose on a gentle spray or a watering can fitted with a rose head attachment and apply about 2¼ gallons (10 liters) each time, watering the soil above the root ball and taking care not to expose the roots. Aim to imitate a gentle shower, allowing the water time to soak into the ground and encouraging the roots to follow it down to lower levels; watering sparingly directs the roots to the surface, where they are in greater danger of drying out. A mulch of bark chips will also help lock the moisture into the ground.

Regardless of their age, trees in containers require regular watering, especially during the growing season.

POTTED TREES

The exceptions to the two-year watering rule are trees that are planted in containers. These will rely upon you for all their moisture requirements, because their roots, unlike those of trees planted in the ground, cannot access moisture present in a larger expanse and depth of soil. You will therefore have to water your containerized tree throughout its life, especially during the growing season from early spring to fall. To prevent the tree from becoming waterlogged, ensure that the pot has plenty of drainage holes in the base and raise it up on pot "feet" so that any excess moisture can easily escape.

TOP TIP WHEN WATERING, IF THE MOISTURE DOES NOT DRAIN AWAY WITHIN TEN MINUTES, YOU MAY BE OVERWATERING, AND THE SOIL COULD BE IN DANGER OF BECOMING WATERLOGGED, WHICH CAN LEAD TO THE ROOTS AND TRUNK ROTTING. APPLY SLIGHTLY LESS SO THAT ALL THE WATER DRAINS AWAY WITHIN THIS TIME FRAME.

MULCHING MATTERS

Although trees planted in the ground may not need extra fertilizer (see right), applying a mulch can improve the soil structure (see p.27), making water and the nutrients dissolved in it more freely available for the roots to absorb. Add a 2in (5cm) mulch of seasoned bark chips on the soil over the root area, leaving a gap around the trunk. If you are not planting in a lawn, lay the same depth of organic matter, such as well-rotted compost or manure from a farm or stable that does not use chemical pesticides, over the soil beyond the root area. The bark chips are not as absorbent as compost and will therefore be drier and less likely to rot the stem, but they decompose very slowly, while the compost or manure will improve the soil at a faster rate, so this combination provides the best of both worlds for the tree.

Add a bark mulch, leaving a space around the stem. Landscape fabric will also help keep the weeds at bay around it.

FOOD FOR ALL

Research by the Royal Horticultural Society in the UK shows that few garden soils lack key plant nutrients, which means that your tree will probably not require feeding if it is planted in the ground. However, you will need to administer additional nutrients to trees in pots every year. In early spring, carefully remove the top layer of potting soil from around the tree, taking care not to damage the roots. Add an all-purpose controlled-release granular fertilizer at the rate recommended on the packaging to potting mix and use it to fill in around the tree. Alternatively, apply a liquid feed, such as seaweed fertilizer, at regular intervals throughout the growing period, again checking the packaging for the rates and timings of applications, which may differ by product.

Remove the top layer of potting mix in spring and replace with fresh potting mix and granular fertilizer.

PRUNING TREES

Pruning has several important functions, such as removing dead and diseased wood that could result in an infection spreading to the whole tree. Misaligned stems and those that are causing an obstruction across a path, for example, should also be taken out. Some fruit trees are cut annually to encourage them to develop more fruiting stems, while the regular pruning and training of others can create beautiful structural features, such as lollipop-headed bay trees, pleached hedging (see p.19), and multi-stemmed coppiced hazels, which are cut to the ground every year or two.

Removing some lower limbs from a Himalayan birch will reveal more white stems and allow plants to grow beneath it.

WHAT TO PRUNE

A tree that fits your space comfortably when mature will rarely need pruning. However, young trees may require formative pruning (see p.129), and those you inherit or specimens that have become misshapen due to environmental factors, such as shade from a nearby building, may require a trim to maintain a balanced canopy. Also, look out for dead or diseased growth, which should be removed promptly to prevent infections from spreading to the rest of the tree. Fruit trees also require regular pruning, which helps encourage heavier crops by allowing light to reach all the fruiting stems (see pp.130–131).

CUTTING TIMES

Most deciduous trees are pruned from early winter to early spring, when they are dormant. The bare branches allow you to see the structure of the tree clearly at this time of year and to identify crossing branches that can cause lesions, opening the plant up to infections. The exceptions to this rule are members of the *Prunus* genus, such as cherries and plums, which should be pruned in summer. These trees are prone to a fungal disease called silver leaf and bacterial cankers, which are more prevalent in the fall and winter.

Prune evergreen trees, such as *Magnolia grandiflora* and hollies, in late spring if no birds are nesting and trim conifers in late summer.

Most deciduous trees are pruned in winter, when they have lost their leaves and you can see the branches clearly.

Employ a qualified tree surgeon to carry out pruning on large trees or any work that involves using a chainsaw.

CALLING IN THE EXPERTS

Scaling a ladder to prune a tree can be extremely dangerous, so tackle only easy-to-reach branches and stems yourself. Major restorative work or pruning above head height to reach tall branches are jobs for the experts. Contact a qualified tree surgeon or an arborist—ask if they are a member of a professional organization and check that they have insurance before employing them. Also, check how the pruned wood will be removed—if you have no side access, it may have to come through your house.

The stems of pollarded willows (*Salix*) are cut back in spring
to one or two buds above a clear trunk to produce this effect.

MAKING PRUNING CUTS

Learning how to make good pruning cuts will help you keep your tree healthy and productive. Check that you have the right tools for the job, choosing those designed to cut through the width of the stems you wish to remove. When you have mastered a few key pruning techniques for your tree, you can then apply them to other large woody plants in your garden, such as shrubs and climbers.

Make sure that your cutting tools are sterilized and sharp before you begin any pruning work on a tree.

MAKING A CUT

When making a pruning cut, use the appropriate tools and ensure that they are sharp and clean before you start. Cut just above a bud (a slight swelling, bump, or darker line on a stem) or side stem. Where the stems are arranged in opposite pairs, make a straight cut just above them; for others, cut at an angle so that rain will drain away from the bud, preventing it from rotting. Do not prune too close to a bud, which may damage it, or too far up the stem because this may cause the wood between the cut and the bud to die back.

Make a straight cut above a pair of opposite buds.

Make a slanting cut above alternate buds so rain will drain away from them.

TOOLS AND SAFETY EQUIPMENT

Using the right tools for the job will help ensure a clean cut and rapid healing. A basic tool kit will include a pruning saw, ideal for hard-to-reach stems; a bow saw for cutting large branches; and a pair of ratchet anvil loppers, which will slice through stems of about 2in (5cm) with ease. Pruners are ideal for smaller stems of about pencil width or less. Never use a chainsaw yourself—this piece of equipment requires professional training to operate safely. Always wear gloves and protective goggles to prevent debris from damaging your eyes when working at or just above head height.

Cleaning your tools before you begin pruning and again afterward will help minimize the spread of diseases from tree to tree. Dip the blades in a sterilizing solution—products for cleaning babies' bottles are ideal—before you begin cutting. After pruning, run the tools under a tap to remove dirt and then give the blades a rub with wire wool to take off sticky sap. Wipe off any remaining debris with a clean cloth and apply some lubricating oil, such as boiled linseed oil, to prevent rusting.

A bow saw is suitable for large, heavy branches; always wear gloves when using one to prevent injury.

REMOVING A BRANCH

To remove a tree branch, cut it in stages to prevent tears and to make a clean final wound that will heal quickly before infections can take hold. Smaller stems of pencil thickness or less can be removed in one go, following the advice in Step 3.

YOU WILL NEED Sterilizing solution • Robust pruning gloves • Pruners • Pruning saw • Loppers

1 Sterilize your pruning tools before you begin. Then, remove about 2ft (60cm) from the end of the branch with pruners, a pruning saw, or loppers, depending on the thickness of the stem. Continue to reduce the length of the branch, cutting it in a series of manageable sections, until you are about 2ft (60cm) from the trunk or a main stem. This technique prevents heavy branches from tearing close to the trunk or a main stem, which could seriously damage the tree.

2 Next, make a cut in the underside of the branch about 8–12in (20–30cm) from the trunk, stopping when you are halfway through it. Make another cut slightly farther away from the trunk to meet the undercut. This will remove the branch safely and, again, prevent tearing, which could damage the bark and the phloem and xylem beneath it (see p.11).

3 To finish, make a clean, angled cut just beyond the crease in the bark where the branch emerged from the trunk. If the branch is wider than about 4in (10cm) in diameter, make an undercut first and an overcut to meet it to prevent tearing.

4 Do not cut flush with the trunk—the tissue in the collar helps the wound heal, and the small stump will soon shrink back as the tree forms a layer of protective bark over the cut. Do not apply a wound paint, unless cutting a *Prunus* tree, where it may help prevent silver leaf disease.

TOP TIP SUCKERS, WHICH ARE THIN SHOOTS THAT ARISE FROM THE BASE OF THE TREE OR A LITTLE FARTHER AWAY FROM THE TRUNK, TAKE ENERGY FROM THE MOTHER PLANT AND NEED TO BE REMOVED. TRY TEARING THEM OFF, AS CLOSE AS POSSIBLE TO THE ROOT FROM WHICH THEY ARE GROWING, OR REMOVE THEM WITH PRUNERS.

SHAPING A TREE

To minimize the pruning needs of your tree, select one that naturally develops the outline and height you require. Choosing the right tree for your needs is important because pruning may not alter its shape and habit in the long term, especially once it has reached maturity, and it is likely to keep reverting to type a year or two after each cut. An easy way to increase the light below a tree is to "raise the crown," which simply means removing the lower limbs to create a longer clear trunk—but take care not to create a top-heavy crown, which may destabilize it.

Pruning a tree when it is young will encourage it to develop a beautiful balanced shape.

SHIFTING SHAPES

Trees that develop a beautiful outline as they grow will require very little pruning once they have become established, but some formative pruning of a younger tree will help create

Gently pull or tear off young shoots from the main trunk of your tree as soon as they sprout to keep it clear.

a balanced shape with a single clear trunk, if that is what you want, and a strong, healthy canopy.

You can also encourage a young tree to develop more than one trunk if you prefer; this will help restrict its height and keep it more compact as well. To do this, prune the topmost stem, known as tip-pruning, which will encourage buds to shoot farther down it. You can leave a few to grow on, but check that the tree maintains a balanced shape and remove any branches that are likely to make it lopsided, which increases its susceptibility to falling in a strong wind.

As a tree grows, it will inevitably develop some side-shoots low down on the main trunk, which if left will develop into full-sized limbs. Check for these new shoots in spring and summer. The best and easiest way to remove them is simply to pull them off with your fingers as soon as you see them. If you don't spot them until they are larger, cut the stems off with a sharp pair of pruners. Also, take out similar small shoots sprouting from other limbs, which may cause tangled or congested growth if they continue to develop and grow.

COMPETING LEADERS

The leading stem controls the growth and shape of the tree, and if another strong shoot threatens to compete with it, your tree may become misshapen. Remove the weaker shoot and allow just one leader to prevail. If the leader of a tree with opposite shoots has been damaged, it will form a forked pair of stems. In this case, again remove the weaker and tie the remaining leader to a vertical cane to train it to grow upright.

Where two stems are competing, remove the weaker to leave one leader to grow on.

FORMATIVE PRUNING

If you buy a standard tree from a nursery, it will be a few years old and will probably have already undergone some formative training to produce a clear stem (or a few stems, if you have bought a multi-stemmed specimen) and a balanced canopy. Younger feathered whips, which are cheaper and often sold as bare-root plants (see p.30), will be unpruned and will require a little initial work in the first few years to establish a balanced shape.

Immediately after planting, remove any damaged stems, together with any that are crossing or rubbing others. Do not prune the leader, which is the main stem at the top of the tree, but do remove any side stems (laterals) that are growing unevenly up the leader. Aim to establish a straight main stem and a set of well-positioned laterals that will all receive light. At this stage, leave some laterals, known as "stem builders," on the lower half of the tree; their leaves will help feed the plant during the spring and summer, providing energy for it to grow and establish.

In the second and third years, continue to remove some of the lower stems from the leader and any other awkwardly placed branches or thin, weak growth. Also, prune out any strong stems at the top of the tree that may compete with the leader, which could result in an unbalanced canopy shape (see opposite). If growth is weaker on one side of the tree, prune the tips of the branches on that side, which will promote stronger, thicker growth.

Prune the tips of a holly to encourage more stems to shoot farther down the stem, resulting in bushier growth.

PRUNING EVERGREENS

Evergreens, such as hollies and strawberry trees (Arbutus), have a dense canopy of permanent leaves, which can become quite heavy, especially when laden with snow in winter. It is therefore best not to create a top-heavy crown on a long, clear trunk, which may be more susceptible to snapping during a strong wind. Instead, allow a balanced network of stems to develop lower down the trunk, which will help stabilize the tree and protect it from wind damage. Remove any dead, diseased, weak or uneven growth, pruning from late spring to late summer, but check that you will not disturb any nesting birds before doing so.

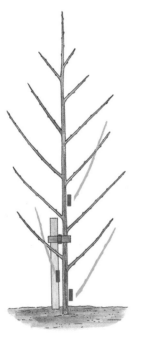

Year I: Remove laterals growing unevenly or those that threaten to rub against stems farther up the main stem.

Years 2 and 3: Remove laterals from low down on the main stem and those farther up that are spaced unevenly.

RENOVATING AN APPLE TREE

Pruning an established fruit tree will help encourage new growth and ensure that all the stems receive adequate air and light. An airy, open canopy will be less susceptible to disease, while light stimulates the flower buds to open and the fruits to ripen. Your aim is to create a balanced shape that will also help stabilize the tree. You can prune a small tree yourself, provided you will not need a tall ladder to reach the top branches; for a larger specimen, avoid accidents by calling in a professional tree surgeon.

WHEN TO PRUNE AN APPLE TREE

Trained fruit trees such as cordons are best pruned in late summer to create fruiting spurs because you can see the basal leaves at this time of year (see p.37). Freestanding apple and pear trees are pruned in winter, when the leafless network of branches is exposed. It is also a good time to renovate an old tree, such as the one shown here.

PRUNING METHOD

Before you start, collect your tools, such as loppers, a pruning saw, and pruners, making sure that they are all sharp and clean.

1 Start by looking over the tree for dead stems, which will look darker in color and snap easily. Remove these at the base. Also, take out any that show signs of disease, such as fungal growths, orange or black spots, or scarring. Use the correct tools for the size of branch (see p.126).

2 Take a step back to check for crossing or rubbing stems and remove these, cutting them back to a main branch or the trunk. Thin out young shoots that would cause congestion if left to mature. Keep in mind that each fruiting stem must have sufficient light for the apples to swell and ripen.

3 Take each section of the tree in stages, removing stems that will impede light falling on the flowers and fruits. Try to create an open framework, especially in the center of the tree, where the stems often become crowded and unproductive.

4 Take out a few older branches to make way for new growth, but do not prune too heavily, which would promote a lot of leafy growth the following year. The foliage feeds the tree but forms at the expense of flowering and fruiting stems.

A well-pruned apple tree will be laden with fruits in early fall, providing a bumper harvest.

TREE PESTS

Pests that attack trees come in all shapes and sizes, from large mammals such as rabbits and deer that are easy to spot to tiny insects responsible for damage that may only become apparent once the tree is infested. A healthy, mature tree will generally sail through minor incursions by insect pests, but a good bill of health will not necessarily save them from more deadly types. When trying to remove pests from your tree, avoid using chemical pesticides because they may also harm beneficial insects, such as bees, as well as pest predators, including ladybugs and hover fly larvae.

Knots of twiggy growth, known as witches' brooms, are caused by gall mite activity but do little harm to the tree.

PROTECTION AGAINST PESTS

Pests that attack trees can be found in almost any yard, and insects that fly in will be almost impossible to deter, but taking a few precautions can minimize the risk of an attack and help prevent a full-scale infestation. The first step is to check new trees for signs of pest damage; a reputable nursery should offer a guarantee and replace any pest-damaged specimens.

Planting your tree properly (see pp.34–35) and keeping it watered while it establishes will help ensure strong, healthy growth, enabling it to ward off serious attacks by many pests. Most will do minimal damage to a mature tree, and although a few holes in the leaves may look unsightly, they will have little effect on its overall growth. Remember, too, that many pests provide an important food source for other insects and birds (see *opposite*) and form part of the yard's ecology, so it may be best to tolerate them if their activities are not too harmful.

Planting a tree in the right soil so that it establishes well and produces healthy growth will help it ward off pest attacks.

Check your tree in spring and wipe off any pests, such as aphids, before an infestation causes distorted leaves.

REGULAR CHECK-UPS

One easy way to keep pest damage to a minimum is to check your trees regularly and to diagnose and treat any serious problems that arise. If you spot just a few pests munching on your tree's foliage, and you can reach them, try picking or wiping them off. When numbers are quite small, this is relatively easy and may stop the pest in its tracks; insects such as aphids often focus on young leaves and stems, so pay special attention to these in spring.

BARRED FROM ENTRY

Large pests, such as deer and rabbits, will eat both the stems and foliage of young trees, which can kill them if the damage is severe. If rabbits have access to your yard, fit a specialist guard around the tree trunk at the time of planting and check and loosen it as the stem grows. Deer are more difficult to control because the larger species can reach up into the canopy and tear off branches as well as gnaw the bark when food is scarce in winter. Install a tall barrier designed for deer protection around the tree if you cannot fence off the entire yard to keep them at bay.

Deer eat shoots, leaves, and bark; protect your tree from attack with a tall guard that keeps them at a distance.

Ladybug larvae consume aphids that suck the sap from young tree foliage.

BRING IN PREDATORS

Birds eat a variety of insects, beetles, and worms, including some tree pests, picking them off the branches and buds and helping keep the plant healthy. Some insects are also pest predators; for example, the larvae of ladybugs, lacewings, and hover flies all consume woolly aphids (see p.135). A few types of wasps eat tiny pests, such as leaf miners, which are the larvae of various moths, flies, sawflies, and beetles that burrow into foliage, while birds and other garden creatures, including spiders and earwigs, eat the adults. The best way to maintain a thriving predatory army is to avoid using any pesticides in the garden.

STICKY SITUATIONS

The caterpillars of winter moths (see p.135) eat the developing fruit buds of such trees as apple, plum, pear, and cherry, but you can control them by applying grease bands or tree barrier glues (horticultural grease) around your tree. These sticky products prevent the wingless females from climbing up the tree trunk and laying their eggs. Place the grease bands or glues on trunks and tree stakes about 18in (45cm) above soil level in mid-fall, before the adult moths begin to emerge later in the season. Reapply if the bands lose their stickiness and keep them in place until mid-spring when the activity of these pests declines.

Apply a grease band around your apple or pear tree to prevent winter moth caterpillar damage.

Oak processionary moth caterpillars are a danger to humans as well as trees.

CHEMICAL ATTACK

Chemical pesticides are rarely required on ornamental or domestic fruit trees, and the choice of products for sale is now very limited because many have been banned due to the environmental damage they cause. Organic pesticides based on natural pyrethrum, fatty acids, and plant oils do not contribute to chemical pollution levels, but they also target beneficial insects such as bees, so use them carefully.

Some pests that pose a more serious risk, such as oak processionary moth (OPM), require removal by trained professionals. Call your state agricultural extension service if you find this pest on your oak tree.

IDENTIFYING COMMON PESTS

If a pest is damaging your trees, first try to identify which one is causing the problem by looking through the descriptions and symptoms listed here, which represent some of the most common types. Many pests will inflict only minor damage, and you may not need to take any further action, or you can allow the pest predators in your garden to do the work for you (*see p.133*). However, a few may need to be removed if your tree or crops are more seriously threatened; always use organic methods that will not affect the other wildlife in your garden.

ADELGIDS *ADELGIDAE* SPECIES

Similar to aphids but often covered with a white waxy substance, various different types of adelgids suck the sap from a range of conifers, including larch (*Larix*), spruce (*Picea*), and Scots pine (*Pinus sylvestris*). They may also produce galls (small round growths) on young shoots. In the case of the spruce, these little insects produce swellings that look like tiny pineapples.

CONTROL Although the waxy coating and galls may look unsightly, these insects do relatively little damage, and because there is no effective control for large trees, they should be tolerated. If you can reach the adelgids on smaller trees, try squashing them or wiping them off with a tissue. Also, encourage pest predators such as ladybugs into your garden (*see p.133*).

Adelgids are tiny creatures similar to aphids; look out for their white, waxy coating.

CODLING MOTH *CYDIA POMONELLA*

Caterpillars of the codling moth cause maggoty apples and can also affect pears and, occasionally, walnuts and quinces. You may spot a little hole in the fruits where the small brown-headed white caterpillar has crawled out before it turns into a moth. Affected fruits also tend to drop early.

CONTROL If only a few of the fruits are affected, you may wish to take no action. For heavier attacks, try a biological control of pathogenic nematodes, which are minute wormlike creatures that kill the caterpillars. Spray the trunk, branches, and soil beneath the branches in early fall, after the caterpillars have left the fruits, to provide protection the following year. Organic contact insecticides containing pyrethrins may also help control this pest.

Signs of attacks by codling moth caterpillars include dark patches and holes in the fruits.

WOOLLY APHID *ERIOSOMA LANIGERUM*

This sap-sucking insect affects apple trees and is easily identified by the white fluffy coating that the aphids secrete, which may be mistaken for fungal growth. The aphids often attack areas around recent pruning cuts, where the bark is thinner. The affected shoots often look lumpy, and frost may split the wood, opening up the tree to apple canker disease (*see p.139*).

CONTROL These aphids are difficult to control on tall trees, but where you can reach them on smaller plants, scrub them off with a stiff brush in early spring before an infestation develops. Also, encourage pest predators, including ladybugs, the larvae of lacewings and hover flies, earwigs, and the parasitoid wasp *Aphelinus mali*, which keep these pests in check.

The woolly coating secreted by these aphids is often mistaken for a fungal disease.

BAY SUCKER *LAURITRIOZA ALACRIS*

These plant suckers feed on the foliage of bay (*Laurus nobilis*) during the summer months. The nymphs cause rolled and distorted leaf edges; the foliage then turns yellow as the pests suck out the sap. You may also see the small grayish-white insects underneath or near the curled leaf edges.

CONTROL The distorted growth on your bay tree looks more harmful than it is; in most cases, bay suckers do not impede the overall growth of the plant because they affect only half of each individual leaf. Check your tree from spring onward, and if you can reach affected leaves, simply tear them off with your fingers or use pruners. Also, encourage predators, such as birds, ladybugs, wasps, and ground beetles, which eat the nymphs.

Bay suckers cause rolled leaf edges on bay trees during the summer months.

WINTER MOTH *OPEROPHTERA BRUMATA*

Winter moth caterpillars eat holes in the leaves, blossoms, and developing fruits of a range of deciduous trees and include the mottled umber moth (*Erannis defoliaria*) and March moth (*Alsophila aescularia*) as well as *Operophtera brumata*. The moth caterpillars affect many ornamental deciduous trees as well as apples, pears, plums, and cherries. Severe attacks can weaken young trees and affect fruit crops.

CONTROL Tolerate caterpillars on ornamental trees because the leaf damage does not affect their overall health. On fruiting trees, try applying grease bands or tree barrier glues (*see p.133*). Also, encourage pest predators, such as birds; the caterpillars of these moths provide an important food source for birds when they are nesting.

The tell-tale signs of winter moth caterpillar attack are small holes in the foliage.

BROWN SCALE *PARTHENOLECANIUM CORNI*

A tiny sap-sucking insect, brown scale affects many woody plants, including *Cotoneaster* species and plum trees. You can identify it by the hard brown shell-like bumps, about ⅛–¼in (3–6mm) in length, that collect in groups on the stems. A black sooty mold may also develop on the sugary honeydew they excrete. A heavy infestation may affect the healthy growth of a tree.

CONTROL Light infestations do little damage to mature trees, and populations are often kept in check by ladybugs, parasitoid wasps, and some birds. If your tree is suffering a heavy attack, try to wipe off the adult scales and eggs. Organic sprays based on natural pyrethrum and fatty acids may also help control the nymphs when they are active in summer.

Sap-sucking brown scale looks like hard, shell-like bumps and distorts growth.

GALL MITES *VARIOUS SPECIES*

The presence of these microscopic animals, also known as eriophyid mites, is usually only obvious when a tree develops abnormal plant growths in response to their feeding activities. The creatures suck sap from their host but also secrete chemicals that cause growths, or a "gall," to form. The mites are also sometimes responsible for the formation of witches' brooms, which look like birds' nests. Other symptoms of attack include rolled leaves, patches of hairs or red bumps on the foliage, and enlarged buds.

CONTROL Despite the dramatic symptoms caused by gall mites, the effect on a tree is very minor, and most will continue to grow well, so no control is needed. The mites are also food for other garden wildlife.

The chemical these tiny mites secrete can cause the formation of red pustules on acer leaves.

TREE DISEASES

Trees can be vulnerable to a range of diseases caused by bacteria, fungi, or viruses, especially when they are growing in poor conditions, which reduces their immunity and resistance to attack. Young trees are most at risk, so check that yours are in the site and soil best suited to their needs. Keep them well watered until their roots are established; if the stems or leaves of newly planted trees are wilting, they may be lacking moisture rather than suffering from anything more sinister. Check regularly for signs of diseases and cut out any infected stems to help prevent their spread.

This bay (*Laurus nobilis*) was pruned in the fall, and the new leaves have been damaged by frost rather than a disease.

TOP TIP REDUCE THE LIKELIHOOD OF INFECTION BY PICKING UP ALL DISEASED FOLIAGE AND FRUITS FROM THE GROUND, WHICH MAY OTHERWISE GO ON TO REINFECT YOUR TREE OR OTHERS IN THE AREA.

PREVENTIVE MEASURES

To help keep diseases at bay and reduce their harmful effects, make sure that your tree is planted in the conditions it enjoys. Also, check that you have not buried the stem too deeply in the soil, which can cause fungal infections, such as honey fungus (*see p.138*), to take hold. Watering young specimens regularly and pruning a tree of any age carefully will also help prevent attacks; poor pruning cuts and trimming your tree at the wrong time of year when fungi are more prevalent can leave wounds open to infection. Pruning evergreens in the fall can also stimulate the growth of young shoots and leaves that may be vulnerable to frost damage.

Such diseases as powdery mildew, which causes white powdery patches on leaves, are often caused by dry soil conditions, and although they may affect the growth of young trees that have not been watered consistently, a few infected leaves will not harm an otherwise healthy mature tree.

Keeping a tree in good condition can minimize the effects of most diseases, but some virulent types, such as ash dieback, a fungal disease that kills ash species (*Fraxinus*), will infect even the healthiest. If you have a tree that is afflicted by a serious disease such as this, contact the relevant government authority for advice.

NON-CHEMICAL SOLUTIONS

Many tree diseases cannot be cured with chemical treatments, and the height and width of these stately plants often make it difficult or impossible to apply the few that may have an effect. For most tree diseases, early detection and the removal of any infected parts to limit their spread are the best forms of control. Always clean your tools after pruning out infected growth to avoid transferring the disease via their blades.

After removing infected stems, clean, sterilize, and dry the blades of the tools you have used.

The best way to deal with diseases, such as apple canker, shown here, is to cut out the affected wood as soon as you see it.

RESISTING ATTACK

Some diseases attack specific species of tree, and in many cases it is possible to select a cultivar that has either been bred to resist attack or offers natural immunity. For example, many apple varieties are resistant to scab, a fungal disease that produces scabby marks on the fruits.

If you plan to plant a few trees in your yard, opt for different species or varieties, which will reduce the risk of infections spreading from one to another. You are therefore less likely to lose all of them if a disease does take hold, and the range of species increases the biodiversity in your yard too.

Planting different species in your yard will help limit the spread of disease from one tree to another.

IDENTIFYING DISEASES

Check your tree regularly for signs of disease, and if you see a lesion, spots, or other marks on the stems, buds, flowers, or fruits, check through the descriptions and symptoms here to diagnose the problem. Early detection and the removal of diseased growth can prevent the spread of the infection and more serious harm to the tree. When looking at symptoms, also remember that your tree may be suffering from drought stress or frost damage rather than a disease, so if the former is possible, try watering first to see if that provides the cure.

HONEY FUNGUS *ARMILLARIA* SPECIES

Many trees and shrubs are susceptible to this fungal disease, which kills the roots and ultimately the whole plant. Honey fungus causes a white fungal growth between the bark and the wood, which may crack and bleed close to ground level, as well as honey-colored fruiting bodies that appear on infected stumps in the fall. The disease also causes black shoelacelike rhizomes to develop below the soil surface.

CONTROL There is no cure for honey fungus, and you will have to remove affected trees to prevent its spread to other woody plants. Also, add a vertical barrier to prevent the rhizomes from spreading. Bury pond liner or heavy-duty plastic 18in (45cm) deep in the soil, with about 1in (2–3cm) above the surface, around the area of infection.

Honey fungus is named after the honey-colored fruiting bodies on infected plants.

SILVER LEAF *CHONDROSTEREUM PURPUREUM*

Affecting *Prunus* species, including cherries and plums, this fungal disease causes the foliage to turn a silvery color—hence the name. Fungal growths with whitish woolly upper surfaces, purple-brown below, also occur on dead wood from late summer, and the inner wood of cut stems has irregular dark stains.

CONTROL Prune susceptible plants in summer when fewer fungal spores are around and wounds heal more quickly. If you spot an infected stem, remove the diseased growth before the fungal bodies appear, cutting off the branch 4–6in (10–15cm) beyond the area of infection to healthy wood. Sterilize cutting tools between each cut to prevent reinfection. Burn the diseased stems or take them to a recycling center.

Prune plum and cherry trees in summer when fewer silver leaf spores are around.

FIRE BLIGHT *ERWINIA AMYLOVORA*

This bacterial disease kills the shoots of eating and crab apples (*Malus*), pears (*Pyrus*), and *Cotoneaster, Sorbus,* and *Crataegus* species. The dead shoots look as if they have been scorched by fire, but the first sign may be wilted blossoms in spring, which then die, and a slimy white liquid that seeps from infected stems. The wood also turns a reddish color.

CONTROL Remove all growth showing the reddish-brown staining beneath the bark, cutting stems back 12in (30cm) beyond the infection to healthy wood in smaller branches and 2ft (60cm) in the case of larger branches. Sterilize tools between each cut to prevent further spread of the infection. If possible, also remove infected blossoms and flowers that appear later in spring before they open.

Shoots that are infected by fire blight look as if they have been scorched by flames.

BLOSSOM WILT *MONILINIA LAXA; M. FRUCTIGENA*

The fungal disease blossom wilt affects apples, pears, plums, cherries, and related ornamental trees, killing the flowers, fruiting stems, and small branches. The blossoms turn brown and shrivel, while small, buff-colored pustules form on the dead stems. The same fungus is also responsible for brown rot, which causes similar pustules to form on the fruit, which then rots on the tree.

CONTROL Remove all brown, rotted fruit from the tree and the ground and bury it at least 1ft (30cm) below the soil surface, or take it to your local recycling center and add it to the green waste. Also, cut out and burn infected fruiting stems and blossoms. When buying a new tree, look for one of the cultivars that are resistant to this fungal disease.

Blossom wilt and brown rot produce buff-colored pustules on the flowers and fruit.

CORAL SPOT *NECTRIA CINNABARINA*

A fungal disease that affects many trees and other woody plants, coral spot causes infected branches and stems to die back. Small coral-pink raised spots form on the branches after they have died. The disease often takes hold when a tree is grown in poor conditions or has been pruned incorrectly.

CONTROL Coral spot spreads quickly in wet and humid conditions, so always prune your tree during a period of dry weather. Cut branches through the slight swelling at their base known as the "collar" (see p.127) rather than flush with a stem or branch. Remove dead stems that may be harboring the disease as soon as you see them, cutting back to healthy wood. Also, try to improve a tree's growing conditions to reduce the risk of reinfection.

Cut back tree stems with bright coral-red pustules as soon as possible on a dry day.

APPLE CANKER *NEONECTRIA DITISSIMA*

This fungal disease causes sunken patches of dead bark on apples, pears, and *Sorbus* species and some other trees. The infection often starts on young branches and fruiting stems, and if left, it can kill the area above the infection point. On mature branches, the flaking bark exposes the dead wood in the center of the stem. Fruit may also rot and fall.

CONTROL Canker often occurs on trees grown in wet clays and acid soils, so ensure that your trees have good drainage and do not grow susceptible species in acid conditions (see p.27). Also, look for varieties that offer resistance to canker. Remove affected branches and fruiting stems, cutting back to fresh, healthy growth. Make clean cuts that heal quickly to reduce the risk of reinfection.

Remove stems with dead or flaking bark promptly, cutting back to healthy wood.

BACTERIAL CANKER *PSEUDOMONAS SYRINGAE*

This type of canker affects the stems and leaves of *Prunus* species, such as plums and cherries. Symptoms include sunken patches of dead bark, which may also exude a sticky gum, and small holes in leaves, known as "shothole." Infected stems die off quickly. If the only symptom is a sticky residue bleeding from the stems, your tree may not have canker, so look for other signs too.

CONTROL Prune a susceptible tree in midsummer when the bacteria that cause canker are dormant and the tree has more resistance to attack. If you see a diseased stem, remove the infected area, pruning back to healthy wood and making clean cuts. Burn the prunings or take them to a recycling center. When buying a new tree, choose one with canker resistance.

Bacterial canker causes patches of blackened dead bark and small holes in the leaves.

INDEX

Bold text indicates a main entry for the subject.

Authors Zia Allaway & Holly Farrell

AUTHOR ACKNOWLEDGMENTS

Zia: Many thanks to Paul Reid at Cobalt id for his beautiful design of this book, and to editor Diana Vowles and the Dorling Kindersley team for their help in fine-tuning the words.

PUBLISHER ACKNOWLEDGMENTS

DK would like to thank Mary-Clare Jerram for developing the original concept, Chris Young for content origination, Nicola Powling for jacket development, Margaret McCormack for indexing, and Paul Reid, Marek Walisiewicz, and the Cobalt team for their hard work in putting this book together.

PICTURE CREDITS

The publisher would like to thank the following for their kind permission to reproduce their photographs:

Alamy Stock Photo: A Garden 32tr; Adrian Sherratt 66c, 76bl; All Canada Photos 119tr; Andreas von Einsiedel 18br; Andrew Darrington 38bl; Annette Lepple 19br, 33tr; Art Directors & TRIP 19bl; Avalon.red 15tr, 42bl, 52tr, 134br; Barrie Sheerman 56bl; BIOSPHOTO 12tr, 13bl, 81tr, 94tl; blickwinkel 15br, 16tr, 71tl, 76tr, 82bl, 96bl, 114bl, 131c, 135bl; Bob Gibbons 51tl, 62br; Botanic World 51br; Botany vision 95br; Brian Hoffman 36tr; C J Wheeler 43tl, 44tl; chasephoto 20cr; Chris Baker 17bl; Clare Gainey 68bl, 72tr; Dave Bevan 27tc; Deborah Vernon 16cr, 97bl; DGDImages 124cr; Ellen Rooney 41cl; Florapix 44bl; Flowers and Gardens by Jan Smith Photography 56tr; GardenPhotos.com 54tl; garfotos 12bl; George Ostertag 106tl; GKSFlorapics 48bl; Graham Prentice 122tr; Holmes Garden Photos 61bl, 75tl; HS Floral 46c; Ian Lamond 32b; ian west 123tl; Image Professionals GmbH 2-3l, 22tr; Imagebroker 16tl; Joe 138br; John Glover 102c; John Martin 73bl; John Richmond 10br, 63br, 98tl, 113bl; K.D. Leperi 21bl; Kay Ringwood 34cl; Klaus Steinkamp 79tl, 99tl; Leonie Lambert 101tr; Lesley Pardoe 109bl; m.schuppich 115bl; Mabo 6c; Marcus Harrison - plants 112bl; Martin Fowler 79br; Martin Hughes-Jones 52bl, 58br; Matthew Taylor 90br; mauritius images GmbH 115tr, 134bl; McPhoto/Rolf Mueller 62tl, 95tl; Michael Preston 19tl; mike jarman 64bl, 109tr; Minden Pictures 133cr; Mode Images 29c; Müller / McPhoto 57tr, 89tr; Nature Picture Library 45bl; Nigel Cattlin 14cl, 84bl, 137tl; O.D. vande Veer 107br; P Tomlins 78br; Panther Media GmbH 2c, 139br; Paul Thompson Images 88bl; Perry Mastrovito 9tr; Peter Malcolm 41bc; PjrNature 33bl; Prf_photo 108bl; R Ann Kautzky 101bl; Rachel Husband 42tr; Real Gardens / Stockimo 49tr; RM Floral 74tl; Robert Schneider 28bc; roger tillberg 110c; Rufus 117br; shapencolour 8bl, 10cl; simon leigh 137br; Steffen Hauser / botanikfoto 45tr, 50tl, 99br, 119bl; Steffie Shields 59tl; STUDIO75 77bl; The National Trust Photolibrary 12br, 102cl; thrillerfillerspiller 65bl, 72bl; Tim Gainey 54br, 59br, 86c, 92tr, 93bl; 96tr; Tony Watson 69tr; Val Duncan/Kenebec Images 132tr; wda cache 105tr; Westend61 GmbH 40bl; Wiert Nieuman 38br, 68tr; Wirestock, Inc. 15tl; Zena Elea 13br; Zoltan Bagosi 116br.

Dorling Kindersley: 123RF.com: Leonid Ikan 20tr; 123RF.com: xalanx 132bl; Alan Buckingham 84tr, 85bl, 126bl, 130c, 138bl, 139bl; Brian North / RHS Chelsea Flower Show 2010 22cl; Brian North / RHS Hampton Court Flower Show 2012 24c; Brian North / Waterperry Gardens 38tr; Cambridge Botanic Gardens 14bc; Debbie Patterson / Ian Cuppleditch 23cr; Dreamstime.com: Lihana 23tr; Dreamstime.com: Susan Mcarthur Letellier 133tr; Dreamstime.com: Whiskybottle 138tr; Mark Winwood / Dr Mackenzie 44tr; Mark Winwood / Marle Place Gardens and Gallery, Brenchley, Kent 69bl; Mark Winwood / RHS Wisley 9tl, 14bl, 17br, 27cl, 28cl, 34tr, 41tr, 48tr, 60tr, 71br, 80bl, 91tl, 105bl, 107tl, 114tr, 125c; Peter Anderson 20bl, 40tr, 55br, 57bl, 103bl; Peter Anderson / RHS Hampton Court Flower Show 2014 21tr; RHS Wisley 16br, 98br.

GAP Photos: Graham Strong 78tl; John Glover 77tr; Liz Every 91br; Maddie Thornhill 53tr; Martin Hughes-Jones 60bl, 94br; Nicola Stocken 93tr; Richard Bloom 118tr; Visions 80tr.

Getty Images: fotolinchen 90tl; Meinrad Riedo 70tl; Nahhan 117tl; Neydtstock 26tr; patty_c 50br; rob2211 113tr; Sergio Amiti 100bl.

Illustrations by Debbie Maizels & Cobalt id.
All other images © Dorling Kindersley

DK | Penguin Random House

Produced for DK by
COBALT ID
www.cobaltid.co.uk

Managing Editor Marek Walisiewicz
Editor Diana Vowles
US Editors Heather Wilcox, Megan Douglass, Lori Hand
US Consultant John Tullock
Managing Art Editor Paul Reid
Art Editor Darren Bland

DK LONDON

Project Editor Amy Slack
Editor Lucy Sienkowska
Senior Designer Glenda Fisher
Managing Editor Ruth O'Rourke
Managing Art Editor Marianne Markham
Production Editor David Almond
Production Controller Stephanie McConnell
Jacket Designer Amy Cox
Jacket Coordinator Jasmin Lennie
Art Director Maxine Pedliham
Publisher Katie Cowan

First American Edition, 2023
Published in the United States by DK Publishing
1745 Broadway, 20th Floor, New York, NY 10019

Copyright © 2023 Dorling Kindersley Limited
DK, a Division of Penguin Random House LLC
23 24 25 26 27 10 9 8 7 6 5 4 3 2 1
001-333483-Mar/2023

A catalog record for this book is available from the Library of Congress.
ISBN: 978-0-7440-6965-5

Printed and bound in China

For the curious
www.dk.com

MIX
Paper | Supporting responsible forestry
FSC™ C018179

This book was made with Forest Stewardship Council™ certified paper—one small step in DK's commitment to a sustainable future. For more information, go to www.dk.com/our-green-pledge.